John Vickers

The crucifixion mystery

A review of the great charge against the Jews

John Vickers

The crucifixion mystery
A review of the great charge against the Jews

ISBN/EAN: 9783337148126

Printed in Europe, USA, Canada, Australia, Japan

Cover: Foto ©Lupo / pixelio.de

More available books at **www.hansebooks.com**

THE CRUCIFIXION MYSTERY.

A REVIEW OF THE GREAT CHARGE
AGAINST THE JEWS.

JOHN VICKERS,

AUTHOR OF THE "NEW KORAN," "THE REAL JESUS," ETC., ETC.

WILLIAMS AND NORGATE,
14, HENRIETTA STREET, COVENT GARDEN, LONDON;
20, SOUTH FREDERICK STREET, EDINBURGH;
AND 7, BROAD STREET, OXFORD.

1895.

WYMAN AND SONS, LIMITED,
PRINTERS,
LONDON AND REDHILL.

CONTENTS.

INTRODUCTION, p. xi.

Rational work, and irrational conduct.—Antiquated moral exemplars.—Rationalism relies not wholly on reasoning—Salutary religious illusions.—Childish minds require authoritative guidance.—The modernising of ancient authorities.—Revolts from authority lead to some moral laxity.—The harmonising influence of public worship.—Associative illusions and others.—Rational teaching must condescend to the popular intelligence.—The educational work of preachers and editors.—The difficulty of diffusing book instruction.—Rationalistic literature studied, by Christian ministers.—The Crucifixion charge previously considered.—Jewish reasons for avoiding controversy.—Dr. Priestley's "Letters to the Jews."—The Anti-Conversionist Society.—A prospective "amicable discussion."

CHAPTER I.
THE NAKED IMMOLATION,

§ 1. *Pictures and Narratives*, p. 1.

Ideal sketches, pose drawings, and drawings from nature.—Unnaturalness of the Crucifixion narrative.—Hence supposed by some to be an ideal sketch.—Why the representation can be best explained as a dramatic scene.—Objections anticipated.

§ 2. *Some Sacrificial Theories*, p. 11.

Complex character of the Crucifixion.—Lord Beaconsfield contends that it was no crime.—The Rev. Dr. Bartle affirms that Christ was necessarily the author of his own death.—These theories, while they tend to clear the Jews from guilt, are totally at variance with the Jewish religion.

§ 3. *Origin of Sacrifices*, p. 15.

Tributary offerings of the nature of bribes.—They fall into discredit as people get more enlightened.—Expiatory sacrifices originate from the custom of tribal retaliation.—Children and slaves selected as victims.—People did not immolate themselves till they believed in a future existence.—The Jews only took their own lives when they would otherwise be slain by enemies.—A hypothetical case of Jesus sacrificing himself to save his countrymen from bloodguiltiness.—The immolation at Calvary of an entirely opposite character.

§ 4. *The Schooling of Jesus*, p. 23.

Every teacher must first be taught.—John the Baptist's influence on Jesus.—He is probably moved by dramatic visions to suffer death.—He applies to himself Isaiah's description of the afflicted nation.—He escapes from Ritualists and is captured by Mystics.—Messiah-worship leads to the construction of a new theology.—The Father sacrificing a good Son for his servants' transgressions.—Jesus morally lowered by a mistaken idolatry.

§ 5. *Vicarious Atonement*, p. 34.

Dr. Herman Adler's declarations on the subject.—Demoralising tendency of the superstition.—The unenlightened prefer favour to justice.—All wrong-doing requires correction.—Mr. Gladstone's defence of the doctrine considered.

CHAPTER II.

THE PLAIN PASSION-DRAMA.

§ 1. *Nazarene Asceticism*, p. 40.

The old Jewish doctrine that people are dealt with equitably in the present life.—Origin of the idea that present ills and wrongs are corrected in a future existence.—It induced many to court poverty and pains that they might so become entitled to recompense.—A reversal of human fortunes expected in the Kingdom of Heaven.—Austerities practised by early Christians.—St. Simeon Stylites and others.—Penance made the substitute for persecution.

§ 2. *Assisted Penances*, p. 49.

The crucified Convulsionaries.—Profitable suffering from either friendly or hostile hands.—The Messiah was to be abased on earth or he could not be exalted in Heaven.—The treatment of Jesus outrageous as a punishment, but reasonable as a penance.—A dramatic penance of the Dominicans.

§ 3. *Transfiguration and Trial*, p. 54.

Dramatic action passing for natural action.—Ananias and Sapphira struck dead.—Apparition of Moses and Elias on the mountain.—What the real Moses would have been likely to do on returning to life.—Value of the apparition as a means of conferring on Jesus authority.—His hostility towards those who held a ruling position.—Dramatic acts on approaching and entering the city.—The mysterious arrest.—The rôle of Iscariot.—The trial of Jesus evidently a mock trial.—Remarks of Dr. Benisch and Dr. Geikie on the subject.—Some criticisms of Keim,

§ 4. *The Resurrection*, p. 67.

The greatest Christian miracle losing credit.—On what grounds a general resurrection was anticipated.—Unreasonable demands produce a fictitious supply.—Incompleteness of resurrection miracles.—In the raising of Lazarus and others, no proof of death.—In the rising of Jesus, no proof of identity.—If crucified by enemies, they would not have surrendered the body.—Joseph commanded the garden and all who moved therein.—An exhibition of wounds as vouchers of identity denotes a want of the true natural features.—Theory of a change of clothes preventing recognition.—M. Renan's theory of subjective visions.—The concert of crafty and credulous minds.—Propagandist stratagems of the author of "Daniel," and the rich Arimathæan.

CHAPTER III.
THE CLOAK OF MARTYRDOM.

§ 1. *The Significant Silence*, p. 84.

Mistake of Isaiah as to the suffering of captive Israel, and the further mistake of Christian interpreters.—The slender testimony on which the Crucifixion charge rests.—The inference now drawn from the silence of contemporary writers in reference to the accompanying prodigies.—Had the Calvary transaction been a great public spectacle it could not fail to provoke wide and general comment.—Jews and Romans silent respecting it.—Forged testimonies of the third century.—What Josephus says of Pilate's procuratorship.—The Samaritan accusation.—The Pilate of the Gospels and Christian legends. —His report of the Crucifixion spurious.—A genuine report, having so much value as a controversial weapon, would not have been allowed to perish.—How Pilate would have acted had he known of the proceedings at Calvary.

§ 2. *Character of the Accused*, p. 96.

The evidence of character in criminal charges too much overlooked.—The Evangelists weighed against the Jewish Sanhedrin.—Why the Jews were in bad repute with Greeks and Romans.—The educational work of the Sanhedrin.—That college evidently an improving body.—M. Renan's baseless charges against the family of Annas.—Religious persecution then impracticable.—The Roman toleration.—The alleged "persecutions" in the Book of Acts.

§ 3. *Character of the Accusers*, p. 106.

Christian writers addicted to calumny.—Dean Stanley's remarks on monkish chroniclers.—The early fictionists and mystics.—The canonical Gospels.—Calumnies of the second century.—Diabolism and the martyr-spirit conducive to intolerance.—Persecution considered necessary for the perfection of saintship.

§ 4. *The Prophet-killing Charges*, p. 113.

The Gospels misrepresent Jewish history.—The prophets opposed one another, and were not in general treated unjustly. —The people suffered more wrong from prophets then they inflicted on them.—Sectarian prophets slain in times of religious strife.—Prophets liable to ill-treatment when they became political partisans.—Those who spoke as sages and moral reformers had nothing to fear.—The intemperate declamation imputed to Jesus.

§ 5. *Mythical Saint-slaying*, p. 119.

The massacre of the Bethlehemites clearly mythical.—Conflicting statements respecting John the Baptist's death.—The reasons for which he was probably executed.—The story of Stephen's martyrdom.—The speech ascribed to Gamaliel.—A pretended Gamaliel discovers Stephen's relics.—The mild Herod Agrippa charged with killing the apostle James.—The legendary martyrdom of James the Less.—The alleged crucifixion of Peter, and the beheading of Paul.—Story of St. Mark's cruel death at Alexandria.—Dean Milman on Apostolic martyrdoms.

§ 6. *The Crucified Children*, p. 130.

The conflict between Christianity and Paganism.—When the Pagan population was at length converted, more attention was directed to the Jews.—Why they were supposed to slay children.—Fictitious evidence against them.—St. Simon of Trent.—St. William of Norwich.—Extravagant stories told by Jewish renegades.—The boy flogged to death at Inmestar not a typical case.—Anti-Jewish prejudice partly dispelled by the Reformation.—Incriminating stratagems still practised against them.—The compromising Protestant position.—The mediæval charges compared with those advanced by the primitive Church.

§ 7. *No Motives for Murder*, p. 144

People never band together to take life without strong motives.—Dr. Benisch's remarks on the absurd charge of blasphemy against Jesus.—The supposed hostility of the Jewish sects.—No reason ever given for Saul's furious antagonism.—Dean Milman's attempt to explain the animosity of the Scribes, Lawyers, and Pharisees.—The theory of a great national disappointment.—A warrior Messiah would not have been welcomed at that period.—The Romans could have no better reason than the Jewish authorities for sending Jesus to execution.—Remarks of Dr. Strauss on the alleged influence brought to bear upon Pilate.—A governor, whom bad men could use as a tool, must have been an imbecile.

§ 8. *Clear Motives for Calumny*, p. 153.

The Jewish authorities were a hindrance to Nazarene proselytism, and could only be discredited by calumny.—Fiction and the drama as instruments of sectarian slander.—All rival sects resorted to defamation.—Canon Robertson on the false charges made against the early Christians.—The advantage which

Christians had over Jews in the conflict of aspersion.—Godfrey, the "Protestant martyr."—The martyr-stratagem of Grangeneuve and Chabot.—The sacrifice of Jesus under a cloak of martyrdom.

§ 9. *The Betraying Manner*, p. 167.

Real crimes distinguished from fictitious crimes by their studied secrecy.—The false charges against the Jews, and the Grangeneuve plot thus betrayed.—The Athenian Council's treatment of Socrates.—Had the Sanhedrin condemned a popular teacher to death it would not have been by crucifixion.—Assassination the usual method of unscrupulous rulers for getting rid of dangerous opponents.—The enemies of Jesus could not have crucified him without encountering strong opposition.—The apology now made for his friends and disciples in not trying to save him.—They simply acted in accordance with his wishes.—For the Jewish rulers to have crucified him it would have been an act of madness: for the Nazarenes it was an act of astuteness.

§ 10. *The Conclusion*, p. 175.

With the progress of enlightenment the alleged wickedness of the Sanhedrin is becoming unbelievable.—Why the charges were not long ago refuted.—*The Jewish Chronicle's* remarks on the Crucifixion calumny.—The good work that is being done by liberal Christian ministers.—Dean W. H. Fremantle on the friendly relationship of Jews and Christians.—The Crucifixion solemnities still kept up in some churches.—The retrogressive teaching of a recent tale entitled "Barabbas."—Its gross exaggeration of the ancient calumnies.—The strong Anti-Jewish prejudice instilled by such fictions.—Enlightened Christian poets might embellish the Life of Jesus in another direction.

INTRODUCTION.

Rationalism, at which so much undeserved abuse has been hurled during the last half-century, is only another name for wisdom; so long as people take reason for their guidance, they are wise, and when, prompted by some fancy or impulse, they begin to act against the dictates of reason, they are unwise. All men while skilfully following their industrial avocations may be considered good Rationalists; the gardener, the carpenter, the tanner, the weaver can give a sound reason for every step they take in carrying on their work. They seldom make any serious mistake in their operations, and they are generally very teachable; if anyone can point out to them a more advantageous method of proceeding, they will be found ready listeners and not at all backward to follow good advice.

It is highly desirable for human welfare that we should not only have rational work, but rational conduct; if people would everywhere live in accordance with reason, as they are accustomed to labour, we should have no vice and crime in the world, no calamitous quarrels, no wastefulness, and no extreme want. Unfortunately, a large number of our fellow-creatures have never had a true industrial apprenticeship; others have been trained to earn a living, but have not been trained to live, and they cease to act wisely the moment they get away from their business, or lay down their tools. The groom, who has been tending his horses rationally with every consideration for their health and comfort, will not give the same wise attention to himself; the ploughman, who has been at great pains to draw a straight furrow, will not pursue an equally straight course among his fellow-men; the mason, who has studied uprightness in putting one building stone to another, will not, by adding act to act in the establishment of his own character, seek to attain a corresponding consistency and rectitude.

In conduct, as well as in art, people profit from the teaching of experience, and grow wiser and better as they advance in years, so long as no casualties or deteriorating influences are met with to interrupt this order of progress. Healthy individuals and healthy societies are naturally reformative, ever taking note of the mistakes which have been made in the past with the view to their avoidance in future, ever introducing improved methods and better arrangements into the economy of life. We ought, with increased knowledge, to excel our fathers in all things, and our children will inherit such advantages that they will be under an obligation to do proportionately better than ourselves. Moral excellence does not, however, obtain the speedy recognition which is invariably accorded to technical excellence—a sage is little noticed in his life-time, and when after death he becomes famous, and wide and general attention is directed to him, his teaching will be out of date. Those who want model farmers or model physicians, look round about them with discrimination; but if they are in search of model men, they turn their eyes backward and copy the rude patterns of a bygone age. At an industrial exhibition, there may be arranged in due order the successive improvements which have been effected in the construction of many useful articles during the last two or three centuries. A manufacturer, who inspects them with the view of learning to produce something equally good or better, will pass lightly over the earlier and ruder forms, and concentrate his attention chiefly on the advances which have been made in the latest designs. The literary student, who visits a public library that he may learn to write good poetry, will probably read with esteem Chaucer, Spenser, Shakespeare, and other famous bards who lived long ago; but will take as his models what are generally considered the best poets of the present century. In respect to morals and the conduct of life, however, people generally do just the reverse; they deem the most enlightened and estimable of their contemporaries far less worthy of imitation than the renowned saints and heroes who lived when there was hardly any reliable history, and the world was immersed in superstition and barbarism.

What Rationalism says is this: We should honour our progenitors; we are greatly indebted to those who preceded us; they did much for improving the world before we had any existence. Great respect should be shown for the sages and prophets of old who endeavoured to teach men their duty; some of their noble acts may be imitated now with advantage, and some of their wise sayings are good for all time; but it is an entire mistake to regard them as the best exemplars of conduct on which we can frame our own lives. As they moved forward in their day and occupied fresh ground, we must advance in ours and take up another decidedly reformative position. If we are always looking backward and paying idolatrous homage to those who lived long ago in circumstances very different from our own, as though virtue attained in them its highest perfection, it is a hindrance to human progress. Instead of gazing so long and intently on the commemorative statue, we must give more attention to the good man in the street. A higher general standard of morality would be much sooner reached, if people could only be persuaded to set before them living exemplars, and study in human conduct, as they study in everything else, the latest improvements.

Those who fail in the common duties and obligations of life should be reasoned with, and got into right ways if possible, but Rationalism does not rely wholly on reasoning for the attainment of this object, it adopts any method of checking and correcting erratic tendencies that is found to be effective. The tamer of beasts does not reason with his animals at all, neither does the charmer of serpents—it would be utterly useless to do so; he still treats them rationally, however, and contrives to exercise such a controlling influence as shall keep them from doing serious mischief. There are human beings with such strong animal passions and weak reflective powers that no amount of good counsel will make any perceptible impression on them, or bring them to a sound, rational condition of mind. Music will often have a more salutary effect in soothing or mastering passionate and emotional characters than the most powerful appeals to the intelligence. Other incitements to a reformation of evil habits may be brought to bear on them with great advantage. Those who cannot be reasoned out of their illusions and induced to live wisely, may generally be restrained to some extent, and kept in a safe course, by good counter-illusions, such as have been furnished by religion.

A large number of the inhabitants of this country will be found leading decent lives, not from any real love of virtue, but because they are somewhat superstitious—that is, subject to religious illusions. To take away those illusions, as some have endeavoured to do, and leave them a prey to their selfish illusions, is not to enlighten and elevate them, but the surest means of effecting their debasement. While there is always some hope of reclaiming a superstitious criminal, the sceptical Anarchist, or Nihilist, who thinks that he has a right to make war on society, is as lost to all reforming influences as a fierce, intractable wild beast. Any belief that exercises a wholesome restraint on the passions, and keeps people from committing rash acts or drifting into licentiousness, when their reasoning powers are too feeble for that purpose, may be rightly considered of great value in the economy of human life.

The majority of adult people are in much the same mental condition as children, and require authoritative guidance, as they are not able to reason out a wise and correct course for themselves. And there is no ethical authority that will command wide and general respect, unless it has been long established, so as to acquire an illusory magnitude. It is possible for a reformer to gather a few followers in his lifetime, but he will never come to be venerated by millions as a teacher and exemplar, till there has grown from his initiative, many years after his death, a great, organised community. Hence it is, that the generality of mankind are so prone to look backward in the study of right conduct, and fix their eyes on models that are antiquated. In Turkey and Egypt at the present day, plenty of men may be found superior in moral character to Mohammed; but no one there would be got to believe that they are worthy of being compared with the great prophet. In China, though many persons can be met with more enlightened and wise than Confucius, the multitudes of that country who honour the philosopher would not for one moment allow them to be considered his peers. As there is no means of overcoming this superstition, it is usual for the thoughtful to embellish the character of the popular idol by imputing to him modern ideas, by extolling his virtues as much as possible, and keeping his faults entirely in the background. A thousand organised teachers, thus speaking wisely under one authority, will command greater attention and do far more good in a country than could possibly be effected, if they were scattered loosely among the population speaking every man for himself independently.

People in the transition state of passing away from authoritative guidance, and endeavouring to think and act for themselves, are very liable to go wrong to a certain extent, and commit grave indiscretions. A bold, self-reliant youth, who has recently escaped from leading-strings and does not care a pin what is said to him by his elders, is far more likely to err seriously than a less intelligent but tractable child. Adult persons, who have broken away from their country's established religious teaching to take an independent course, are sure to be for some time in an equally grave and critical position. It has been observed by travellers who visit Constantinople, that the most immoral Turks will be found among the intelligent class who seldom attend the mosques, and are sceptical in regard to the high claims of the Koran. Such people cannot be made simple and credulous again, and their conduct is not likely to improve, but by their gradually getting wiser with experience. A little thinking has led them to disregard the promises and threats held out as incentives to a virtuous life, and a more complete exercise of their reflective powers may be expected to convince them, at length, that it is advantageous under any circumstances to keep in the straight path of purity and probity.

The revolt against marriage obligations, now generally deplored, and the licentiousness of such men as Byron and Burns, are often very unjustly ascribed to Rationalism. In reality the moral laxity exhibited by these bold, adventurous characters comes from their not being half rational enough—from their utter inability to acquire a mastery over their passions when emancipated from superstitious fears. If due attention were given to the teaching of Rationalism, more social restraint would be put on the pairing of the unfit, and there would be very few hasty and thoughtless unions of the incompatible, so that matrimonial squabbles and divorces would be of more rare occurrence. The dreamy views promulgated by some modern novelists in regard to sexual relationships have found favour with a certain portion of the readers of light literature, but they are not likely to be entertained by rational minds in this or any other country. The institution of marriage can only be consistently assailed by such teachers as Rousseau, who think that it would be advantageous to abolish property and family, so as to reverse the great march of civilisation and return to the primitive equality of savage life.

One serious charge against Rationalism is that it tends to dissociate people, to detach them from religious fellowship, and scatter them loosely as individuals to study their private interests free from all sympathy or sense of obligation towards the rest of the community. It is only a semi-rationalism that produces this result; those who become half-enlightened are very much inclined to part company with the ignorant, but when once they get more enlightened they are more condescending and disposed to care for the improvement of their benighted fellow-men. If people were all equally wise and moral, it would not much matter about their assembling every week in churches and chapels for public worship, they might get on very well as good neighbours in their separate homes. It so happens that they differ widely in character, in intelligence, and in circumstances, and to get them to live harmoniously when so diversified, it is of immense importance that they should meet from time to time as a great family under one roof to pray and sing together, to hear the same admonition, and be subjected to the same harmonising influences. An enlightened man, though he may not get much instructed or elevated himself in a congregation, will attend public worship, when he can conveniently do so, for the good of his wife and family, or the benefit of the surrounding community. Doctrinal and other reforms may suggest themselves to his mind as being desirable, but he will not expect such reforms to be introduced, till the want of them is felt by a majority of the population when they have reached a higher standard of intelligence. One less enlightened and rational studies himself alone, and unless a religious service is conducted in such a way as to exactly accord with his tastes and ideas, he will have no part in it. The very ignorant, who might be beneficially instructed and morally elevated at any church or chapel, are accustomed to stay away from selfish motives, sometimes wasting their hours at gambling and other low diversions. There is as much difficulty in inducing them to assemble regularly for goodfellowship and wholesome instruction as in getting children to attend a Sunday school. As reasoning will not avail much to bring the inhabitants of a district together for the improvement of their conduct and the bettering of their relationships, some other means may be legitimately adopted for that purpose, even if it be of the nature of an illusion.

Ignorant, selfish people, under the influence of some illusion, have occasionally been got to associate and form an important community, when nothing else would have moved them to live and act together for their mutual welfare. The belief entertained by the early Christians, that the end of the world was near, produced some evil consequences; it suspended industrial operations to a certain extent, and brought a number of mistaken people to great poverty. But the world never saw anything to be compared to it as a powerful inducement to voluntary association; thousands of scattered individuals ceased to study any longer their domestic affairs and other private interests, and rushing together to be in readiness for the crack of doom, became a permanent religious brotherhood. When the Church was thus constituted, education was possible; the more thoughtful and intelligent members became teachers, and the more ignorant learners, and the gradual improvement of the collective body was rendered inevitable.

Some forty years ago a similar illusion, industriously promulgated by the Mormon prophets, achieved what no amount of reasoning or persuasion could have ever effected as a great constructive social force. According to their interpretation of Nebuchadnezzar's dream (Dan. ii. 34), the breaking of the image by the stone cut out without hands, signified the crumbling of all the Gentile nations before the growing kingdom of Latter Day Saints. Their elders proclaimed this new belief as a warning with so much zeal and earnestness to the ignorant people whom they collected on our village greens, that a considerable number of frightened peasants were induced from year to year to leave their doomed country, and hurry westward to the Salt Lake Valley that they might escape the impending destruction. Once arrived at their Land of Promise, they were set to work directly in reclaiming the wilderness, and they became in a little while such a successful colonial community that they were not greatly disappointed at the fulfilment of the predictions being long delayed, nor disposed to regret the scare which had started them away from their old homes.

Belief in the efficacy of curative charms, whether for freeing the body from disease, or the soul from sin, is an illusion which affords consolation to rude, ignorant, imaginative people. When they might have been in a condition of utter despondency from the pains, worries, and troubles which sadden their lives, such a belief reassures them, and fills them with hopefulness. Strong, persistent faith on the part of the superstitious sufferer is known to have in certain cases a decidedly ameliorative influence. But those who trust in miraculous remedies for every human ill, are not likely to get a thorough knowledge of the laws of health, and adopt in consequence such wise modes of living that they may successfully ward off infirmities. In proportion as the imagination is brought under control, and correct thinking causes charms of every description to fall into discredit, there will be observed a decided improvement in the physical and moral condition of mankind.

While some religious illusions are decidedly beneficial to weak minds, and deserve to be upheld on rational grounds, and others, if harmful to a certain extent, produce also good results which ought to be recognised, a third class are the reverse of beneficial; so far from contributing to the moral improvement of people, their effect on human conduct is wholly injurious. Such, for instance, was the ascetic mania which caused so many ancient saints to retire into the deserts and afflict themselves with frightful austerities, in the hope of earning thereby compensation in Heaven. Such was every outbreak of fierce intolerance which imprisoned and burnt conscientious men as dangerous heretics because they were unable to conform to the orthodox standard of belief. Such, too, was the senseless war against witchcraft which consigned a large number of inoffensive people, whose only fault was eccentricity, to a cruel death. And if these hurtful superstitions have nearly or quite disappeared from the world, others still linger among us to the prejudice of true religion, and are likely to linger till the general population shall attain a higher degree of enlightenment.

Salutary illusions, if necessary for a time, are sure

to give way eventually to the growth of intelligence, and must not be relied on as permanent incentives to right conduct. Those who live virtuously only from fear of punishment, or hope of reward, or respect for authority, should be taught, as far as it is possible to do so, that it is highly advantageous to cultivate virtue for its own intrinsic worth. But the world is a great university, containing many classes and various grades of learners, and all cannot be expected to profit alike from the same course of instruction. If we attempt to force on people more advanced and rational teaching than they are prepared to receive, they will be sure to turn away from it, and the efforts which we have directed towards their improvement will be vain and purposeless.

Not long ago, I had some friendly intercourse with a party of Salvationists, after writing a few letters in their behalf, and rendering them other trifling assistance. I felt much respect for the people, as they had reclaimed some bad characters, and were carrying on a considerable reformation movement in the locality with small means. The only Rationalistic instruction which I ventured on giving them was to this effect: "Don't you think that more good might be done by going about your work a little more quietly, so that you might not stir up angry passions and provoke bad men to acts of violence? I believe the General would be of that opinion. As soldiers you are bound to contend against every kind of wickedness, but it is possible to carry on a very effective moral warfare which will not provoke physical-force retaliations. Many poor ignorant fellows now regard you as enemies; you want to make them see clearly that you are their true friends—that you fight not against them, but only against the bad habits that are injuring them. Some think it a great honour to be knocked about and maltreated in a good cause; it is really more honourable to teach rough people in a way that they shall not lose their tempers, and get in such a mad state of mind as to commit acts of gross injustice." This bit of counsel was well received by them, and seemed likely to have some permanent moderating influence. But had I gone further, and criticised their doctrine and discipline in a Rationalistic spirit, not the slightest good impression would have been produced on them, and they would have ceased to regard me as their friend.

I have recently attended several different religious services — Episcopalian, Presbyterian, Unitarian, Congregationalist, Methodist, Baptist—and have been on the whole very pleased with the pulpit discourses there delivered. The ministers seemed to me to be doing their best to enlighten the people who came under their influence, and make them more rational. Many wise utterances came from their lips in reference to our common life-troubles which were worth remembering, and might be equally well laid to heart by the learned and the ignorant. They endeavoured to set forth clearly the duties which different classes of the community owe to one another. The evils resulting from commercial dishonesty were in one or two instances ably exposed. And it appeared to be the general aim to recommend virtue in such a way that no one, by losing the fear of Hell, should be tempted to lapse into licentiousness. If such teaching is steadily persisted in, and people can be got to renounce their evil habits and follow higher rules of conduct, a revision of prayers and hymns will presently be called for, as they will not go on for ever believing the irrational and immoral doctrines inherited from a barbarous age.

It is an excellent educational economy which enables people holding different religious views to receive instruction every week at their respective churches and chapels without confusing and interrupting one another. A minister, with a few hundred sympathetic people before him, is encouraged to do his best, knowing that what he says will be so well received, that no groans and hisses will be raised to jar with his discourse. He exerts himself, therefore, to good purpose; his flock are much enlightened and benefited, and the outside and uncongenial public go about their business uncomplaining, well beyond the reach of his voice. Teaching a congregation in this way, is like drilling seed into a well-cultivated field, where every grain may reasonably be expected to germinate and become productive. A similar economy may be witnessed on a larger scale in the regular distribution of our periodical literature; the editor, as well as the preacher, has his established connection; every newspaper and magazine is sure to give swift satisfaction to a large number of readers, because it falls into precisely the right hands, and does not offend the rest of the community. Imagine all our journals, with their various religious and political views, getting into wrong hands for once. Instead of universal satisfaction being afforded the reading public, there would be terrible imprecations and outbursts of wrath throughout the country, enough to raise the roof of Heaven.

It would be well if new books could be distributed in the manner of periodicals—sent off at once to a number of sympathetic subscribers so as to afford profitable instruction to many, and give nobody the slightest offence. Except in very rare instances, it is utterly impossible to do this. Books of a reformative tendency, designed to teach and not merely to amuse, are got into circulation slowly and with much difficulty. Not only is there necessarily great delay in their distribution, but in endeavouring to accomplish this ignorantly and awkwardly by the only means available, they are pretty sure to fall to some extent into wrong hands. A poor book-writer, going forth to teach at a venture, is likely to labour with as little economy as the sower in the parable advancing on waste ground. What with stones, thorns, birds, and other obstructions, only a small portion of the seed which he scatters can be expected to reach a congenial soil, and even some of that not directly or so soon as could be desired. Judging from my previous experience with new books, there are two classes of complaining readers to whom it will be well to apologise beforehand in regard to the distribution of the volume which is now being introduced, namely; those who will get it in good time, and dislike it on finding that it does not accord with their views; and those who will heartily approve of it, but get it late, and wonder that there was not more advertising, bell-ringing, and trumpet-blowing commotion to direct their attention to it. There is really no help for these failures to send book-instruction promptly to precisely the class of minds who are likely to appreciate it without causing the rest of the world any annoyance.

It will probably be said by some readers of the present volume, that I am acting unwisely, as an educationalist, in writing at all a controversial work which so entirely conflicts with long-established popular belief. But there have been published to good purpose plenty of other books which must be considered on that score equally objectionable. Those who wish to commune with a few thoughtful minds, have no need to defer saying what can be profitably said because they happen to be in the presence of the unthinking multitude. When our conversation is of such a nature that it should not come to the ears of children, I believe that it is possible to talk quietly over their heads. The periodical literature which deals with such subjects as "Evolution" and the "Higher Criticism" is regularly and widely circulated in this country, and read with much interest by those who are prepared for it, while the bulk of the population go on amusing themselves with their pretty stories and bits of news, and are wholly unconscious of its existence. This advanced teaching will, however, get more extensively diffused in time. If the vast majority of our fellow-men are quite incapable of grasping it now, they will gradually get more reasoning power, and come to accept it eventually. When the sun rises in a mountain country, it gilds at first a few lofty scattered peaks, it next reaches the lower elevations, and after awhile casts its gloom-dispelling radiance into all the deep valleys. In much the same way Rationalism may be expected to gradually illumine mankind, advancing from higher to lower, and still lower ranges of intelligence. It should be a steady, quiet, progressive change, overspreading the world without any violent commotion, without tempest or tumultuous strife.

Rationalistic literature is read at the present day with much interest, not only by those who are thoroughly in accord with it, but by many educated people who can scarcely be expected to view it with approbation. In the libraries of some studious clergymen, will be found the principal works of Darwin, Huxley, Strauss, Renan, Emerson, Froude, Seeley, Morley, Lecky, and others. They like to know something about modern philosophical opinions which differ more or less from their own. It is quite right that they should, and in this way they probably get some enlargement of mind and liberality of spirit. It is not to be expected that they should sympathise much with the free handling of what they consider holy vessels. And having to administer consolation to many weak-minded people in sickness and death, they know, as practical men, that the old superstitions are far more effective for this purpose than the finest teachings of philosophy. Still, if a few sturdy thinkers can dispense with beliefs which are dear to the multitude, and conduct themselves wisely on other than orthodox lines, they see no reason to entertain the slightest feeling of anger or alarm. As it is notorious that arguments against any ancient and generally received doctrine will not be read by the great mass of the people, it does not seem to them necessary to write a single line for the purpose of their refutation. The best Christian Evidences that can be produced in these days are good Christian works, and not crooked, apologetic discourses designed to show that the Church long ago had a supernatural origin, and received direct messages from Heaven. Pride of ancestry is a very poor recommendation for either individuals or communities, especially if it implies an inglorious degeneracy: we must be judged not by what we once were, but by what we are.

Several Christian ministers have, quite unexpectedly to me, read the "New Koran," and expressed a very favourable opinion of its ethical teaching. One of the principal aims of that book was the removal, to some extent, of the obstinate prejudices which tend to alienate Christians from Jews. A study of the terrible Easter charges which used to be brought against the Jews during the Middle Ages, convinced me that they all had their root in the great Crucifixion charge of the first century. Instead of the Jewish people having a fiendish propensity to shed innocent blood from generation to generation, it became very clear that the fault was on the other side—their religious opponents were addicted to calumny. Since the Reformation this has been admitted to a certain extent. Protestant writers are now accustomed to propound some such theory of compromise as the following:—"There is no doubt that in the first century the Jews were real devils, capable of perpetrating any enormity. And the Christians at that period had intercourse with angels; they were genuine saints whose every word may be relied on as strictly veracious. We are thus bound to believe, that what the Evangelists tell us of the diabolical wickedness of the seventy elders in their treatment of Jesus, is throughout pure, unvarnished truth. After the first century, however, the character of the Jews greatly improved; they lost their bad malevolent spirit; they ceased to perpetrate fiendish atrocities, and became as harmless and well-conducted as the rest of mankind. On the other hand, the character of the Christians proportionately deteriorated; they fell away from the original sanctity, and got so corrupt that the angels at length ceased to visit them, and they were no longer inspired, nor empowered to work miracles. Then, seeing the miserable bankrupt condition into which they had fallen, they endeavoured to keep up appearances and maintain their credit before the world by resorting to every species of falsehood and trickery. As they had no real miracles to present to the people, they set their ingenuity at work to furnish a substitute, and continually introduced counterfeit wonders to impose on the credulous multitude. And finding it now impossible to advance a genuine charge of devilry against the Jews, they resolved to make a show of being on the high level of the primitive saints in this matter also, by trumping up against the rival community fictitious charges of guilt, which served as an excuse for remorseless persecution and wrong."

I could not accept this Protestant theory which ascribed to the two peoples such a marvellous change of character in opposite directions. If Christianity became doctrinally corrupted in advancing from

Jerusalem to Rome—a necessary result of continued proselytism—it did not suffer at the same time a great moral declension. Augustine was as good a man as Paul, and the Apostle to the Gentiles was not inferior in intelligence and conscientiousness to the earlier Apostles. Instead of the Christians morally deteriorating as they acquired further culture and a larger experience, they really exhibited from age to age some very decided marks of improvement. It seemed to me quite clear that the pristine excellence of the first century was purely imaginary, that the apostolic church, now invested with such a halo of sanctity, was quite as much addicted to calumny as the mediæval church, and that no reliance whatever could be placed in the unsupported charges of preternatural wickedness which it hurled against the Jewish authorities. In the "New Koran" this was very plainly stated, and it was set forth as a duty incumbent on modern Christians to humble themselves before God, and express sorrow and contrition for the slanders which were propagated by their less enlightened spiritual ancestors. I have since maintained the same opinion in the "Real Jesus," and still more recently in three articles contributed to the *Free Review*, the columns of which were open to a reply. In the following work it has been found necessary, as the result of further study, to modify and revise to some extent what was thus written; the main argument, however, as a vindication of the elders of Israel, is not weakened in consequence, but considerably reinforced.

In recent discussions having reference to the origin of Christianity, modern Jews have been treated by M. Renan and others as a *quantité négligeable*, and it has been quietly assumed that the Satanic wickedness of their ancestors is a historical fact of which there can be no reasonable doubt. It is to a great extent their own fault that they have been thus slighted, for they might obtain a hearing now, and are entitled to have a strong voice in the matter after being compelled for so long to keep silence. They are quick and ready enough to defend themselves against Anti-Semitic agitation and aspersion; to the Herr Stockers, the M. Drumonts, and the Goldwin Smiths that assail them, they will be always found to make a spirited reply. But, with a few exceptions, they have been singularly backward and lukewarm in defending their religious position; they have not spoken out boldly, and to the best of their ability, as Unitarians and other Protestant bodies have done in vindication of their nonconformity. This is partly due to their more serious divergence from the dominant faith, and their recollection of its cruel intolerance, but chiefly to their having long since renounced proselytism. There is a general feeling among them, that they have nothing whatever to gain by entering the arena of religious controversy and demonstrating the correctness of their views in the face of opponents. They rather fear that such a course, instead of raising them in the world's estimation, would be only calculated to inflame the Christian multitude, and rouse against them the terrible hatred and prejudice from which they suffered so much in past times.

Previous to the Reformation, the Jews were compelled at certain seasons to attend Christian churches and listen in silence to sermons there preached for the purpose of effecting their conversion. Protestants ceased to drive them into churches periodically, but established proselytising missions to worry and reproach them; and it would have been thought as shameful a thing on their part to say a word in justification of their unbelief as for a drunkard to speak in defence of his drunkenness. The celebrated Dr. Priestley, in his " Letters to the Jews inviting them to an amicable discussion of the Evidences of

Christianity" (1787), was the first Christian minister to treat them honourably as men entitled to contend freely in behalf of their convictions. He was not only willing to meet them fairly in argument, but was prepared, as a Unitarian, to make important concessions to them, and advance to a considerable extent towards their own position. Had the late Dr. Benisch been his contemporary, a discussion between them of much permanent value might have been expected to result. The two Jewish scholars who courageously replied to his "Letters," though possessing much shrewdness, were inferior to him both in ability and in charity, one of them even descending to vulgar chaff. They did not seem to perceive that their generous opponent was their friend, and proceed in a courteous spirit to take advantage of the excellent opportunity which he afforded them of clearing their community from undeserved obloquy. Moreover, the Rev. Anselm Bayly, a London clergyman, was provoked to step in as a champion of orthodoxy; in a pamphlet bearing on the controversy he belaboured both parties with much warmth, even threatening Mr. David Levi, if his "audaciousness" in reference to the Messiah worshipped by Christians was repeated, to "tear him to pieces." It thus became pretty evident that people's minds were not prepared for the calm consideration of statements at variance with their ancient faith; the time had not come for an amicable and profitable discussion between the two communities which Dr. Priestley so much desired.

In Priestley's town, Birmingham, there was formed in 1871 a Jewish society for defensive purposes, that is, for resisting by argument the attacks which were periodically made on their community by Conversionists. When a missionary from the London organisation next arrived in the town, it was announced that he would preach at St. Asaph's church a sermon of special interest to Jews, who were earnestly invited to attend. From seventy to eighty members of the new society accepted this invitation, and shortly before the commencement of the service marched into the church with their hats on, as they were accustomed to do in their own synagogue. They listened to the sermon with great attention, and at its close the preacher was respectfully challenged by the president of the new society to a public discussion. The challenge was accepted, and a discussion, in which two controversialists on each side took part, soon afterwards came off in the town. But this spirited policy of the Anti-Conversionists did not command the approval of the Rev. S. J. Emanuel, the minister of the Birmingham synagogue. He thought that such discussions were likely to provoke an angry feeling against the Jews, and thus do more harm than good, and through his influence the society was in a little while dissolved by mutual consent.

The good Birmingham rabbi acted wisely on this occasion, with the view to maintaining peaceful relations between the two communities. It was all very well that a discussion should take place, but not with open doors and in the hearing of the prejudiced multitude. The Jews were unlikely as controversialists to obtain a fair verdict from a city population of which they formed but a small minority. Had the points of difference been discussed in the presence of a small select audience, fairly representing both sides, there could hardly fail to have been produced, as a result, mutual respect and mutual enlightenment. A few liberal Christian ministers are known to be on visiting terms with Jewish rabbis at the present day; they are seen to meet occasionally and converse together with the greatest cordiality. Why is this, but because there have been friendly discussions between them on the origin of their differences? And while still holding opposite views they have learnt at least to have a good opinion of one another. But if they assembled ruder minds to form an audience, if they called their respective congregations together and endeavoured in their presence to overthrow each other's arguments, it would more probably lead to a riot than to a reconciliation.

A revival of Dr. Priestley's attempt to arrange "an amicable discussion" between Jews and Christians might be very well made at the present day in the columns of one of the monthly Reviews which furnish a platform for the free statement of all honest beliefs. Certainly no people are more entitled than the Jews to speak out plainly in defence of their convictions, after having to submit for so many centuries to an enforced silence. They are well disposed to forgive past wrongs; there is little doubt that they would write in a more conciliatory tone, and show a greater consideration for Christian susceptibilities than I have cared to do in the course of the following pages. Indeed, unless both parties to such discussion can determine to set forth their views in the most friendly and charitable spirit, no good is likely to result from it, and it will have to be deferred for a time of greater enlightenment. A strong, temperate Jew-Christian controversy, cannot well fail to have the effect of dispelling much ancient prejudice, and bringing about a better understanding between the two communities. There would be nothing to complain of in respect to fairness when a full and free expression of opinion was given from both sides. It is only because these equitable conditions, which are so essential to the proper settlement of a question, have hitherto been wanting that the present work is written.

JOHN VICKERS.

St. Thomas's Hill, Canterbury,
    September, 1895.

THE CRUCIFIXION MYSTERY.

CHAPTER I.

THE NAKED IMMOLATION.

§ 1.—*Pictures and Narratives.*

THE account of the crucifixion of Jesus, forming the most striking portion of the Gospel narrative, is something like a puzzling picture which has different meanings for different minds. It is such an enigma as can hardly be found anywhere else in the whole long roll of human history. And the difficulty of rendering it more intelligible by critical light is immensely increased through there being gathered about it a disturbing force of religious emotion which prevents people from viewing it with a calm and clear judgment, as they would do an ordinary historical problem.

We sometimes meet with an old foreign painting, the meaning of which is not very apparent; it represents perhaps a gathering of villagers for some special purpose not clearly manifest. In another instance we may understand the scene thus presented to us on the canvas; we may perceive that it is an arrest, an execution, a penance, a procession, or a sacrifice. But we may still be quite unable to discover the secret of its production; we may be entirely in the dark as to whether we have before us an ideal sketch, a pose drawing, or a drawing from nature. It may be well to know, if we can, whether the artist really witnessed the scene which he has portrayed, or whether it was constructed entirely from his own imagination. And if it is clear that he painted realistically from what he saw in the external world, it may be desirable to find out whether his figures, artfully posed before him, acted merely for the sake of appearance, or whether they acted from natural impulse, and were quite unconscious of being observed. If the picture has no authentic history attached to it, and is left to speak for itself, the particular method by which it was thus produced can only be got at with certainty or probability by very careful examination and searching criticism.

The formation of written narratives is often just as much a mystery as that of the sketches of human life which are presented to us on canvas. We know well enough that some stories are ideal sketches, pure inventions from beginning to end, and that others are throughout faithful descriptions of what actually occurred, while a third class are of a mixed character—partly historical and partly mythical. But we occasionally meet with narratives which puzzle us to some extent—we are unable to say with confidence whether that which they represent as having transpired is fiction or fact. And if we are satisfied at length that what we are reading is fact; if we are assured that the narrator is not inventing scenes, but describing what really came under his observation, we may still be in doubt whether the action which he describes is natural or dramatic. There is one rule, however, in such cases that will generally enable us to make the distinction—nature cannot be unnatural. For dramatic action to be mistaken for natural action, either in pictures or narratives, by critical minds, it must be a very close and clever imitation of nature, and this is seldom accomplished. Now and then we come on a photographic scene where people are engaged in friendly conversation or working at their trades, and from the naturalness of their expressions and attitudes, it is hard to say whether they were posing before the camera or unconscious of being in its presence. The graphic descriptions which are given in some novels, if presented in a detached form, might pass very well for being the work of an accurate newspaper reporter. But most creations of fancy and pose drawings, whether by the instrumentality of pen or pencil, will be found to depart to some extent, if not to an outrageous degree, from the well-known conditions of natural life.

It has long been believed throughout the whole of Christendom that our four Evangelical narratives of the trial and crucifixion of Jesus are what may be called drawings from nature, just as much so as the reports which have come down to us of the suicide of Antony and the assassination of Cæsar. Unprejudiced critics, after much study, have been forced to the conclusion that they cannot possibly be such drawings on account of their glaring unnaturalness. In the first place, there are connected with the Crucifixion a number of stupendous prodigies which, as they excited no universal astonishment in the world and were unnoticed by contemporary writers, can only be regarded as pure myths. It is well known that prodigies are said to have accompanied the death of Cæsar, and his murder, as an historical event, is not in the least discredited by such legendary embellishment. Several modern scholars have been disposed to consider the crucifixion of Jesus a parallel case of crime, added to and enlarged by the immense excitement which it would produce in the popular mind. But we wish to direct attention to this fact, that even when we get rid of the Crucifixion miracles there is not a sober and reasonable narrative left; the whole account of the cruel treatment of Jesus is unnatural, extremely unnatural in its outrageous wickedness. In the age when Christianity arose, as well as in earlier and later times, good men occasionally suffered from violence if there happened to be a conflict raging, and they were as soldiers involved in the dreadful strife. But when Jesus is said to have been crucified there existed profound tranquillity; no storm of civil war or persecution was maddening people and causing them to perpetrate unusual atrocities. It is made out by the Evangelists that he went about doing good for awhile, and then that his countrymen suddenly, without any apparent reason, rose up against him and resolved to put him to death, while only the single voice of a foreign ruler was raised as a protest against their monstrous injustice. Such a unanimous and unprovoked rising against a national benefactor at so short a notice has never been known to occur anywhere else in the world, and the whole conduct of the Jewish rulers, not only in their treatment of Jesus, but in their openly rewarding and encouraging crime, is a reversal of what was usually done by men in their position and directly contrary to all magisterial nature. Those who examine the narratives with critical eyes, therefore, are becoming more and more convinced that in the Trial and Crucifixion scenes natural action is not represented; the whole exhibition of Satanic wickedness savours of human art, and what investigators are now called on to decide is, whether it can be more reasonably explained as an ideal sketch, or as a pose drawing, in either of which abnormal conduct and extravagances calculated to produce a strong impression might be expected to appear.

A number of mythical theories have been propounded in reference to the production of the Gospels; some of these are based on analogies found between certain Christian doctrines and those of heathenism. The most reasonable mythical theory is that advanced by scholars who believe Christianity to be the genuine offspring of Judaism. In the first place, it is notorious that there were produced from time to time in the Jewish community works of fiction which got to be generally accepted as authentic history. Some of these tales, such as Job, Jonah, Esther, and Daniel, were admitted at length to a place of honour among the sacred writings, and are believed at the present day by many millions of people to be strictly narratives of fact. Long before the birth of Jesus there were firmly established in popular Jewish belief, legendary stories of saints being subjected to cruel treatment, as in the instances of Shadrach, Meshech, and Abednego being cast into a fiery furnace, and Daniel into a den of lions. For several centuries after his death, ecclesiastical writers occasionally invented fictitious martyrdoms which obtained general credit in the Church, such as the hurling of the Apostle James from the battlements of the Temple, and the crucifixion of St. Peter. It is evident, too, that the Evangelists were writers endowed with the same creative faculty and influenced by the same spirit, as is plainly shown by their Bethlehem birth legends, and especially by the story of the Massacre of the Innocents. Moreover, the remarkable silence in reference to the crucifixion of Jesus, the fact of there being no contemporaneous mention of it outside the Christian community, which has long been a mystery to inquiring minds, is clearly accounted for on the hypothesis that what the Evangelists tell us of that terrible transaction is entirely a myth.

But this theory, which has so much that is reasonable to recommend it, is defective just here; it fails to explain how it was that belief in the crucifixion of Jesus, as a matter of fact, got to be so firmly established in the primitive Church before any Gospels were written. All legendary martyrdoms that we know anything about had a literary origin, generally long after the period assigned for their occurrence. Some imaginative writer depicted the cruelties which an ancient saint suffered at the hands of a tyrant, and the fiction so produced got to be accepted as an authentic narrative. The fabulous persecutions ascribed to Nebuchadnezzar were not believed in the Jewish community till the Book of Daniel came from the hand of some unknown Maccabean writer about the year B.C. 165. Prior to the production of the story which is prefixed to Matthew's Gospel, nothing was known in the Christian Church or anywhere else about the terrible Massacre of the Bethlehemites, imputed to Herod the Great. Neither had anyone heard about the cruel death which St. Peter and several other Apostles were doomed to suffer, till the inventive Eusebius and his brother chroniclers undertook to give some account of those venerated saints in the fourth century. The crucifixion of Jesus differs from all these cases in its being firmly believed at the period when it is said to have happened, and before the Christian community had any writings; we are consequently led to infer that it was a scene presented to human eyes in some other illusory form than that afforded by literature. The unnaturalness of the transaction, coupled with the fact that it produced a great impression on Christian minds, while no notice was taken of it in the outside world, forces us to the conclusion that the extraordinary spectacle was really a masked drama, provided for select witnesses on the private grounds of Joseph of Arimathæa. "In the place where he was crucified was a garden, and in the garden a new sepulchre " (John xix. 41). There is, indeed, good reason to believe that the account of the mysterious tragedy, handed down to us in the Gospels, is not an ideal sketch, such as that of the second chapter of Matthew, but a pose drawing; the adversaries of Jesus are personated, and dramatic action is described to us precisely as if it had been natural action.

A pictorial pose drawing is frequently met with, but it is comparatively rare that artificial action for the sake of effect is so presented to us in literature, and when it does occur we know that it was not produced under a corresponding artistic arrangement. One who constructs a painting directs his figures to take up certain positions and assume certain attitudes, and proceeds to sketch them accordingly. He and they co-operate to charm people by placing before them a pleasing illusory appearance. Such co-operation is never practised in literature; if a novelist sketches some of his neighbours minutely in a story which he is writing, it is done without informing them or asking their consent. In ancient times when people posed to produce an impressive scene they did not calculate on their actions being reported at all by the pen; they thought not of readers, and only desired to influence strongly those who were present as spectators. A masked drama got up to serve some purpose might have been witnessed by a hundred or more persons without either of them writing a word about it, supposing that they were able, although they would report it orally. Then after the lapse of some years, if a great sensation was produced and a permanent religious movement was seen to result, it would naturally have been considered by those who were literate an event deserving of historical record. Such we believe to have been the origin of the marvellous narrative presented to us by the Evangelists—that of the trial, crucifixion, and resurrection of Christ; dramatic art produced not only the preternatural wickedness of the Jewish rulers, but the subsequent apparitions of the crucified Messiah, after the supposed rising from the sepulchre. What the Greek Mysteries had been doing to form the opinions of the initiated, and especially to strengthen their belief in the immortality of the soul, these Nazarene masked dramas, contrived, as it seems probable, by the rich Arimathæan and other secret partisans of Jesus, did in a more effective manner for the primitive disciples. The simple Galilean brethren beheld the astonishing scenes presented to them, and, believing the dramatic action to be natural action, were moved as though another world had opened before them, were impelled to go on steadfastly in a prescribed religious course, regardless of what was said by men in authority and fearless of persecution and death.

Some good people who cling to what happens to be in vogue will say that while we point to the unnaturalness of the crucifixion narrative, we advance a theory of explaining it, which to their minds seems still more unnatural—unnatural, perhaps, just because it is novel. It will be extremely hard for many to believe that stratagem of any kind was resorted to by those connected with the primitive Church as a means of promoting faith and enthusiasm. A notion is very prevalent, especially in Protestant Christendom, that in the work of proselytising, the saints of the first century acted up to precisely the same standard of veracity as that followed by an enlightened missionary of the nineteenth century. In an age when illusory appearances of one kind and another were constantly employed by religious teachers for the purpose of recommending their doctrines to the credulous, we are told that one small community presented the remarkable contrast of maintaining a scrupulous adherence to truth. Had such an exceptionally high intellectual and moral development really existed at the time it would have amounted to nothing short of a miracle, and we assume that mankind were then, just as much as now, governed by natural laws. Even when the Christian community had overspread the Roman Empire, and advanced greatly in intelligence, expedients were continually adopted for extending the faith which a modern minister would not consider legitimate. Dean Milman, writing of the numerous forgeries concocted by pious men in the fourth century, says: "To deceive into Christianity was thought so valuable a service as to hallow deceit itself" ("History of Christianity," Vol. III., p. 358).

It will probably be said by some that we are exceedingly presumptuous in rejecting the Church's ancient testimony when no contemporary documents which contradict it have come to light, and all that we have to put in its place is merely conjecture. But this is really the only wise course that people can take when they are confronted by a story which they cannot possibly accept as an embodiment of truth. Children and other simple, imaginative persons bring strange reports to us occasionally without any intention to deceive—tell us, perhaps, that they have witnessed something which we consider supernatural, or that they have seen a sensible neighbour do some outrageous thing which we know he would never dream of doing. Feeling sure, in such case, that our informants are mistaken, we begin to ask ourselves how their mistake probably arose—what they must have seen calculated to produce such an erroneous impression on their minds. And in some instances our reasonable conjectures as to what is likely to have been witnessed and misunderstood, or distorted by imagination, may prove with further information to be absolutely correct. Historical investigators may be expected to deal in this way with reports of the same kind delivered long ago by ignorant, fanciful writers, and then accepted without question as true by the credulity of the age. Legendary stories which tell of the founding of cities and the erection of temples in a miraculous manner, however long they may have held their ground without contradiction, are at once set aside by the enquiring archæologist who desires to form a sound opinion as to how they originated.

The Story of Creation as set forth in the Book of Genesis is far more ancient and venerable than the Crucifixion narrative, and at the present day is more widely and generally believed by mankind. But scientific investigators, although valuing it highly as the poetry of a remote time, have been compelled to treat its testimony concerning the formation of the universe and the introduction of organic life as inaccurate and unreliable. Have they found somewhere buried in the earth a superior and more probable story respecting the beginning of things? Nothing of the kind has been discovered or even looked for; all that they have been able to advance themselves in place of the authoritative record is reasonable conjecture. Astronomers, geologists, and biologists have from time to time thrown out suggestions as to how certain familiar objects at a very remote period came to assume their present form and condition. When such theories have seemed reasonable they have obtained a ready acceptance from the more thoughtful portion of the community, and any hypothesis which critical minds have considered unsound has been honestly controverted, while some view deemed more accordant with the known constitution of nature has been propounded in its stead.

§ 2.—*Some Sacrificial Theories.*

Most people can understand the death of Cyprian, the death of Cæsar, the death of Saul, and the death of Socrates readily enough, but it is far less easy to understand the death of Christ. His crucifixion is an instance of religious suffering of so much complexity that it has been made to appear at once an execution, a sacrifice, a martyrdom, a penance, and, above all, a monstrous crime, and when regarded under these various aspects it has generated much confusion of thought and given rise to endless controversy. Several expounders of the mysterious occurrence have endeavoured of late to make it less difficult by simplification. A majority of Christian theologians at the present day are accustomed to represent it as being both a martyrdom and a sacrifice; but some say that it was a martyrdom alone, and others contend that it was purely a sacrifice. The latter, as it seems to us, take the most correct view of the matter, though we are very far from admitting the truth of the orthodox sacrificial theory. For a person in ancient times to die solemnly before high Heaven as a sacrificial victim, it was requisite that he should not be slain by hostile hands, and we are convinced that this condition was fulfilled in the death of Jesus. Christians in general, however, hold the opinion that he was put to death by his enemies, was cruelly murdered in fact, but was nevertheless immolated for the sins of mankind. Lord Beaconsfield denies that the Crucifixion was an act of criminality; he writes as follows:—

" Born from the chosen house of the chosen people, yet blending in his inexplicable nature the Divine essence with the human elements, a sacrificial Mediator was to appear, appointed before all time and purifying with his atoning blood the myriads that had preceded and the myriads that followed him. The doctrine embraces all space and time, nay, chaos and eternity. Divine persons are the agents, and the redemption of the whole family of man the result. If the Jews had not prevailed on the Romans to crucify our Lord, what would have become of the Atonement? But the human mind cannot contemplate the idea that the most important deed of time could depend on human will. The immolators were pre-ordained like the victim, and the holy race supplied both. Could that be a crime which secured for all mankind eternal joy— which vanquished Satan and opened the gates of Paradise?" (BENTINCK, p. 350).

Mr. J. Cohen, in his able work entitled "The Deicides," believes, like most Jews, that Jesus was put to death by the Romans for political reasons; he does not accept the sacrificial theory of Christian theologians, but he shows more fully and clearly than Lord Beaconsfield has done, that those who do accept it cannot with any reason regard the Crucifixion as a crime. He contends that, according to this view, the Jews who took part in the transaction must have been blind, unreasoning puppets, acting from compulsion, obeying a higher will than their own. The Rev. Dr. Bartle affirms that both Jews and Romans were merely sacrificial instruments in Divine hands; they did not put Jesus to death, nor had the least power to inflict on him any injury. He being in reality both priest and victim, voluntarily immolated himself for human salvation.

"It ought," says Dr. Bartle, "to be distinctly remembered and thoroughly engraven upon the mind, that the God who accepted the offerings of the Jewish priesthood was the same God that accepted the offering of Christ. The priesthood of the Old Dispensation, and especially the high priests, were eminent types of Jesus Christ in His capacity of high priest of the New Dispensation. In like manner also the sacrifices were types of the one great sacrifice offered once for all. It required both a *priest* and a *victim* to prefigure our Lord in His full sacrificial character. Why were the priest and the victim both required to prefigure our Lord? Because he had to *kill* and *be killed*. The priest and the victim had to be combined in the one person. If our Lord failed in this particular His priesthood is thereby forfeited and He could never be a sacrifice. . . . . By the actual taking away of life Christ discharged the duties incumbent on a priest, and by losing His life He became a victim or sacrifice for the sins of men. The death of Christ originated neither from internal nor external causes, His human nature being proof against both. Christ was the author and finisher of His own death, and for this reason He is designated, 'the author and finisher of our faith.' The Christian religion depends entirely on this cardinal truth. It is the basis of human redemption and the very life and soul of the Atonement" ("Jesus of Nazareth," pp. 401, 403).

These theories are so far satisfactory that they tend to clear the Jews from the unjust charge of Christ-murder that has brought on their community so much persecution and prolonged suffering, but it is not by any means so good a vindication as they are able to furnish themselves. If a man is accused of murder and subjected to much annoyance in consequence, it is something in his favour if a party of friends come forward and say they are convinced that he slew from no evil intent and only as a soldier acting under superior commands. It will be a far more effective clearance, however, if he is able to bring forward an array of evidence sufficient to convince any unprejudiced mind that he had nothing whatever to do with the alleged murder, that the charge of his having shed innocent blood from the worst possible motives is entirely a calumny. This is what the Jews can do; and, while they are grateful for any friendly feeling manifested towards them by Christian theologians, they reject all sacrificial theories like those propounded by the preceding writers as being wholly inconsistent with their religion.

If the Crucifixion had really been, as Lord Beaconsfield says, "the most important deed of time"; if it had been planned from the beginning of the world, and was of supreme interest to the whole human race, it would surely have been made known to all whom it concerned, proclaimed in every inhabited region, published in every tongue, and the vast majority of mankind would not have been kept for ages in entire ignorance of its having taken place. We cannot believe that Divine wisdom would contrive to have an event of immense significance to humanity witnessed by so few people and reported in such an obscure and unsatisfactory manner, that many diligent seekers of historical truth, after carefully examining what little original testimony has come down to us respecting it, should be seriously led to doubt its occurrence.

When a wise reformer intends some new arrangement or dispensation to take the place of an old one, the latter is at once abandoned and put aside so that there shall be no confusion or misapprehension on the subject. Had the Crucifixion really been a great final sacrifice, designed to supersede the customary temple-offerings, it is presumable that these would have ceased directly, and that the whole Jewish race would have been duly warned and prepared for the important change which was to take place in their religious economy. We know as a matter of fact that they received no warning at all of any such alteration being intended, that the animal sacrifices went on as usual till the third Temple at length fell like the first in the ravages of war; and at that period the crucifixion of Jesus was such an obscure event outside the circle of his own followers that probably not one Jew in a hundred had heard anything about it. The instruction which Jesus gave his disciples respecting the proper offering of sacrifices (Matt. v. 23, 24; viii. 4) is a clear proof that he expected those requirements of the Law to continue in force till the world's end—then supposed to be near—and had not the faintest idea of their being superseded by his sacrificial death. What enlightened Jews contemplated as a prospective religious reform was, not a complete change in their sacrificial system but the abandonment of sacrifices altogether.

§ 3.—*Origin of Sacrifices.*

The great aim of all rude primitive worshippers was to bargain for supernatural favours, and not to amend their lives or seek to attain a higher standard of morality. The offering of tributary sacrifices, so generally resorted to, was very much like carrying bribes to a judge; it was thought that by such means good fortune would be obtained and evil would be averted. It began to be perceived at length, however, that a man's success in any undertaking or prosperity in life depended more on conduct than on anything else; if he acted wisely he generally attained the object which he had in view, while a foolish and negligent course led to his failure. To those who had become so far enlightened God appeared as a righteous Judge, requiting people strictly according to their deserts, and desiring no one to approach him with bribes. Micah and other Jewish reformers declared expressly that it was not sacrifices that were wanted from men in fulfilment of their religious duty, but straightness of life. The teaching of Hillel went in precisely the same direction, he slighted formal observances, and regarded conduct as the essential thing in religion. Jesus, who had been trained to an industrial life, would probably have taken much the same line as a teacher, if he had not fallen into the hands of mystics who determined to make him a suffering Messiah. And then the notion of sacrifices having any efficacy to relieve people from a burden of guilt, or procure them prosperity would soon have been abandoned both by his followers and the rest of the Jews as wholly inconsistent with Divine Justice. Through his immolation at Calvary there was a revival of the decaying belief in charming away sin with an offering of blood; people were taught, like their rude ancestors, to despise moral conduct and rely wholly on the benefits which would accrue to them from the working of a sacrificial miracle.

Expiatory sacrifices are known to have had a low and barbarous origin at a period when general violence prevailed, and there was nothing like a settled government or regular administration of justice. Petty wars were continually breaking out between small rival communities. In a period of comparative tranquillity a straggler was occasionally murdered in some border dispute by one of another tribe. In such case his fellow tribesmen did not make complaint in due form of the wrong that was done, and insist on the offender being punished. They determined to have satisfaction in another way; they watched their opportunity to retaliate, and when the first member of the tribe from whom they had suffered wrong came within reach he was speedily put to death. Such was the mode of making quits in inter-tribal quarrels, and thus some innocent person frequently had to suffer for another's guilt. Even when a system of justice got to be established it was not always strictly just; if an offence was committed, punishment did not invariably fall on the real offender. The satirical author of "Hudibras" makes it appear that such a crooked administration was possible with Christian settlers in America as late as the seventeenth century. He tells us that on one occasion an Indian was murdered by some useful man whom the colonists could ill afford to lose; therefore, to afford satisfaction to the Indians,

"Impartial justice in his stead did
Hang an old weaver that was bed-rid."

In rude times people naturally got to entertain the notion that their tribal deity required satisfaction for wrongs done on the same loose principle. If a blight, a storm, or a pestilence was raging, they felt certain that it was a judgment upon them for some transgression, and that one or more among them must be put to death to appease the wrath of Heaven, lest the whole population should be speedily destroyed. Children or slaves were generally selected to serve as victims, because they could be best spared, and were least capable of making resistance. The feeling existing in the community under such circumstances may be exemplified by the story of the Russian family in a sledge, pursued by a pack of devouring wolves, when one child after another was thrown to the animals, with the view of purchasing for the rest of the household permission to escape. In a time of calamity, when a sacrifice was supposed to be called for, there was not, so far as our information goes, a single instance of a noble-minded man coming forward and offering to lay down his life entirely for the good of others.

In no part of the world were people ever disposed to immolate themselves till a belief in a future state of felicity held out some prospect of their being able to do so with advantage. The Hindoo widow at a very early period volunteered to be burnt on the body of her dead husband in the full assurance of thus going with him directly to a happier state of existence. The Donatists and other primitive Christians who entreated travellers to slay them, and, in the event of refusal, threw themselves from rocks, or rushed into baptismal fires which were supposed to purge away their sins, were not actuated by any worthier motives. In some instances their motives were less worthy; instead of dying to restore broken ties, in the hope of renewing their relationship with a beloved spouse, husbands deserted their wives, and wives their husbands, and hurried out of the world, caring only for the prospect of securing for themselves individually a good position in Paradise. They were bold speculators in laying down their lives with the view to take them again under happier circumstances, but they were not distinguished by strong family affection, and neither were they good citizens, determined to labour ungrudgingly for the welfare of the community.

There are various Gospel texts which plainly indicate that sacrifice was regarded in the primitive Church mainly as a speculative proceeding with the view to individual profit. "There is no man that hath left house, or parents, or brethren, or wife, or children for the kingdom of God's sake, who shall not receive manifold more in the present time and in the world to come life everlasting" (Luke xviii. 29, 30). "If any man will come after me, let him deny himself and take up his cross and follow me. For whosoever will save his life shall lose it, and whosoever will lose his life for my sake shall find it" (Matt. xvi. 24, 25). "I lay down my life that I might take it again. No man taketh it from me, but I lay it down of myself. I have power to lay it down and I have power to take it again." "Except a corn of wheat fall into the ground and die it abideth alone, but if it die it bringeth forth much fruit. He that loveth his life shall lose it; and he that hateth his life in this world shall keep it unto life eternal" (John x. 17, 18; xii. 24, 25).

It is much to the credit of the Jews that, however cruel they may have been in time of war, they gave no encouragement to the sacrifice of human life as a religious performance, whether voluntary or involuntary. If a pestilence or any other calamity fell upon them they humbled themselves in various ways and presented their burnt offerings, but were distinctly forbidden to immolate their own children, as was done by some of their Gentile neighbours. And when the doctrine of a future existence had got to be held by the greater portion of the community, they were not led in consequence to consider it a justifiable policy to shorten their present lives. It was hoped that those who discharged their duty in a worthy manner would prolong their days, and not abandon their friends and rush on death with the view to securing immediately a glorious reward. A good Israelite was not expected to voluntarily lay down his life excepting in the case of being pursued by remorseless enemies so that death at their hands would otherwise be inevitable. Saul, rather than be slain by the Philistines, persuaded his armour-bearer to kill him, or, as another version has it, fell on his own sword (Sam. xxxi. 4; 2 Sam. i. 10). Razias, when pursued by the soldiers of Nicanor and "being ready to be taken on every side, fell upon his sword, choosing rather to die manfully than come into the hands of the wicked to be abused" (2 Macc. xiv. 41, 42). Several cases of self-slaughter under similar circumstances occurred during the cruel persecutions which fell on the Jewish community in mediæval times, and they were perhaps generally prompted by a feeling of national pride. But a good Jew might be induced to sacrifice himself from higher considerations, especially if he was pursued and in imminent danger of being put to death unjustly by some of his own countrymen. In such case he might reasonably be expected to fall on a sword or ask some dear friend to thrust him through, in order to avert a crime or save his misguided and hostile brethren from bringing on themselves the terrible guilt of shedding innocent blood.

We can easily picture to ourselves Jesus being placed in such a critical position by the persistent hostility of some of his countrymen. We can imagine the chief priests and rulers pursuing him like wolves from one town to another all over Judœa, Samaria, and Galilee, while he is not at all solicitous about his own life or the advancement of his fortunes and only desires to save them from the fearful reproach of bloodguiltiness. At length they come upon him by surprise in some obscure refuge while he is sleeping, and before he can fall on a sword, they arrest him and bring him bound to Jerusalem. He is thrown into prison and preparations are at once made to have him formally condemned to suffer death by crucifixion. When the day of his trial arrives he makes an eloquent appeal to the elders of Israel to reflect well on what they are about, to consider themselves and their children, and on no account bring discredit on their honourable council by a hasty and unjust decision. He tells them that if they are fully resolved that he shall die, he does not fear death, yet would rather live longer and be of some use to them, or at least save them from shedding without reason a brother's blood. If die he must, it is better that he should slay himself than allow them to perpetrate a crime which will render them infamous and bring a lasting reproach on the community. He contends that the children of Abraham should not be enemies, but live together as good brethren according to the Law, and proposes that they should humble themselves on both sides and pray earnestly to God for reconciliation and peace. But he entreats them in vain, his pleading is all to no purpose; they take him to the place of execution and, in accordance with their directions, he is actually nailed to the cross. Then, as a last effort to deliver his mistaken brethren from guilt, he entreats one of the servants of Joseph of Arimathæa to thrust him through with a spear, and peacefully expires. Such a death would indeed have been a noble self-sacrifice, and the memory of it in all human hearts at the present day would have appeased many strifes and borne excellent fruit of brotherly affection.

Unfortunately, the laying down of life as a profitable speculation at Calvary was a sacrifice of quite another character, and it has produced widely different moral results. Jesus was not hunted about the country by implacable enemies resolved on his destruction, and so surrounded at length that there was no chance of escape. He might have continued to live among his countrymen unmolested if he had pleased, for he was not a person whom robbers would be likely to assail, and no one could hope to profit an atom by putting him to death. But he had been led to believe that he was spoken of prophetically in the sacred writings as the suffering Messiah, and that it was necessary for him to die as a sacrifice and be buried and then rise again. This strange mystic programme could only be carried out by his own partisans from whom it was derived, and if his immolation had been accomplished by them fairly and honestly, not much harm would have resulted. They probably thought that in such case a scandal would arise and that they would be charged with murder, and they contrived to give his voluntary death, which was really a sacrifice, an appearance of having been brought about by the malice of his enemies. In short, by means of dramatic action, they not only concealed their own guilt, but deliberately sought to incriminate and discredit the Jewish authorities. So far from any generous effort being made to save blind, unreasoning people from drifting into crime, a semblance of outrageous wickedness was cast over a body of counsellors who were as entirely innocent of the death of Jesus as children unborn. And the terrible injustice did not stay there, but continued to pursue in all parts of the world their innocent posterity. Once branded as a wicked, murderous race, anything that was bad would be believed of the Jews, and when they were scattered at length in a weak, defenceless condition, false charges and incriminating stratagems—a worthy offspring of the original plot—were persistently directed against them, and one fierce persecution succeeded another, till more than half the cities of Christendom were stained with their blood.

There is good reason to believe that many worthy sayings which Jesus uttered during his ministry or in the course of his life produced little impression on those around him and were never recorded, or if recorded were afterwards lost. It is probable, too, that he did many wise and benevolent acts which attracted little notice from the ignorant Galilean people, and were permitted to fade from remembrance. If those lost words and acts of the master could now be recovered by some means, with an incontestible proof of their genuineness, they would afford a profitable study for millions of devout people, and would be welcomed with joy and gladness throughout the whole of Christendom. But as for the libellous story of the Crucifixion, with its surroundings of superstition and devilry, and the terrible spirit of vindictiveness which it propagated, it is a sad pity that it was ever written or was allowed to circulate so widely and obtain such an overpowering hold on the most credulous portion of mankind.

§ 4.—*The Schooling of Jesus.*

Every man who sets out on a mission of teaching must himself first be taught; it is indispensable that he should be preceded by tutors in order that he may be followed in a while by disciples. In the biographies of some distinguished persons we are told the whole history of their education from earliest childhood. There is a complete record of the schools which they went to, the successive masters which they were under, the books which especially interested them, and everything else that contributed more or less to the formation of their minds. But a man is often found acting as a teacher and those who learn from him are unacquainted with his history and have not the least idea how he acquired the information and the doctrines which he is desirous to disseminate. Such seems to have been the case with Jesus; those who gathered about him as disciples were interested in what he said, but they knew not how the thoughts which he communicated had been previously imparted to his own mind. Every prophet was supposed to be Divinely illuminated, or to bring a message direct from Heaven; but the Jewish prophets were of various schools, and they borrowed freely the sentiments and expressions of their fellow-men who preceded them just as much as the Greek philosophers. Jesus was no exception from the rest, and we must now endeavour to form an estimate of the educational influences that were brought to bear on him by inference.

It was probably the preaching of John the Baptist that led Jesus to abandon his industrial calling and take to a life of religious poverty in expectation of the end of the world. Others would then deem him worthy to become the suffering Messiah, who, it was thought, must necessarily be one in a very humble condition. It was not so very difficult for an enthusiastic young man at that period to forsake his home and his kindred with the prospect of the Kingdom of Heaven before him; but the wonder is, how he could be induced to sacrifice his life. During the second and third centuries Christians were occasionally found very eager to die when excited by the conflict of persecution; being full of enthusiasm, they cheered one another in the manner of soldiers who are marching to certain victory; they quoted texts from the Gospels, and pointed to the example of their crucified master, whom they expected soon to meet in Paradise. Jesus himself lived in a period of calm; he had no Gospels for his encouragement, and no enthusiastic comrades eager to suffer by his side; he was called on to pluck up resolution and make the great voluntary life-surrendering adventure alone. He was not a person of visionary mind, not one likely to do this under the prompting of a strong imagination, and there is every reason to believe that some of his more crafty partisans schooled and prepared him by illusory appearances to make the first bold precipitous leap of the Christian flock for the chance of gaining a happier existence.

The Mohammedan ruler, Hassan Sabah, trained a number of devotees to do his bidding under every circumstance, and occasionally sacrifice their lives, by introducing them mysteriously to charming scenes which they firmly believed to be supernatural. When a man had been thrown into a deep sleep by a stupefying draught, he was borne away gently and placed in the Garden of Alamut. He awoke in a while and wondered how he came to be in such a charming situation; delicious fruits were growing close at hand, the air was sweet with the fragrance of flowers, and beautiful damsels came to wait on him and bring the best food and drink for his regalement. In a little while he was again sleeping heavily from the effects of a narcotic draught, and was then removed from the garden and carried back to his former position. When he next awoke and gave some account of his marvellous experience, he was assured by Hassan Sabah that there had been thus granted to him a foretaste of Paradise. Whatever dread of death he might have hitherto felt now vanished entirely; he was prepared to go forth on the most hazardous enterprise, and obey any order, though in so doing destruction became inevitable.

Jesus spoke occasionally like a man who was fully assured that he had had intercourse with celestial beings, and was ready in consequence of what he had thus heard and seen to lay down his life. And he was not subject to trances, so far as we can judge his constitution of mind; the visions presented to him must have been as strictly objective as those which Hassan Sabah's devotees beheld at Alamut. We should be disposed, from the tone of his discourses, to infer that he had been influenced strongly by dramatic apparitions, if there had been nothing else revealed to suggest this belief. But we find in the Gospel narrative some clear intimations that such was really the case. On one occasion some of the disciples were permitted to be present at an interview which he had with two men professing to be Moses and Elias on a mountain in Galilee. They are said to have spoken to him there on the great undertaking for which they were sure to be desirous of preparing his mind—" his decease which he should accomplish at Jerusalem " (Luke ix. 31). They no doubt assured him that he would soon come to life again, as they themselves had done, that he would only be in the grave for three days at the utmost. He therefore felt encouraged and went on to Jerusalem with the disciples, fully resolved to lay down his life. When the time at length approached for finally deciding to die on the cross, his heart somewhat failed him and he was exceedingly agitated with an internal struggle of conflicting desires. We are told that there now very opportunely "appeared an angel unto him from heaven, strengthening him" (Luke xxii. 43). This statement is deemed by some critics a mythical accretion; but white-robed angels, or what passed for such, were occasionally seen in Judæa without any effort of imagination, even as objective ghosts appear now and then in England, and it is probable that the one mentioned here was a fellow of those who were afterwards posted at the empty sepulchre. At any rate, there was good reason for such a messenger to present himself to Jesus on this occasion. It is evident that he was all along being schooled for death by dramatic apparitions, and the rich Arimathæan's Garden of Gethsemane was, in respect to some of its mysterious occupants and the purpose which it was made to serve, very much like the Garden of Alamut.

Jesus was further induced to believe that he was spoken of as Messiah in the Scriptures, and must necessarily die as a sacrifice for their fulfilment. He would not have entertained such a notion of himself, nor could it have been instilled into him by any learned Israelite who had studied the sacred writings to good purpose. The idea of a man being put to death as an expiation for sin was much more in accordance with heathenism than with Judaism. The Jews believed that any guilt for which blood must be made to flow to appease the wrath of Heaven could be transferred to a fit animal by simply laying hands on its head. They considered it altogether wrong to sacrifice innocent children, yet, when greatly provoked in a time of war, had no scruple about putting them to death. They believed, too, that the sins of people were rightly visited on their posterity, even for many generations.

Gradually, however, they became more enlightened and had higher moral conceptions; it was said at length, " the son shall not bear the iniquity of the father; neither shall the father bear the iniquity of the son; the righteousness of the righteous shall be upon him, and the wickedness of the wicked shall be upon him " (Ezek. xviii. 20).

We know that people even now sometimes have to suffer for the faults of others; it is not right that this should be, but it does now and then happen in the world's rough, complicated struggles. When some unforeseen trouble or disaster has occurred, we occasionally hear it said that this or that person has been made a scapegoat of; on him there has been cast an undue share of blame that those who are really most responsible for what has happened may escape censure. No enlightened Jew or Christian would now think of saying that God punishes one man for another's transgressions; when an innocent person does suffer for his neighbour's misdeeds, it is invariably ascribed to human injustice. But the Jews in a barbarous age imagined that God sometimes made scapegoats of people, and many of them imagined they were being chastised for the sins of the Gentiles rather than for any fault of their own when they were conquered by the Chaldeans and carried away into exile. Isaiah of Babylon, in his great Restoration poem, makes the Gentiles acknowledge that such was really the case. " He was wounded for our transgressions, he was bruised for our iniquities . . . . the Lord hath laid on him the iniquity of us all " (Isaiah liii. 5, 6). The unknown writer little imagined that this figurative language which he was making use of would be supposed by some who read in future years to refer to a suffering Messiah, and would induce an enthusiastic Jew in that character to offer himself as a sacrifice.

In the time of Jesus three widely different religious schools existed—the Ritualists, the Moralists, and the Mystics. If he had fallen into the hands of the Ritualists they would have made him a slave of routine and ceremony; he would have been required to do certain prescribed acts at certain times with an utter disregard for circumstances. And strict sabbath-keeping, or rigid fasting, or unreasonable scruples with regard to diet might have completely ruined his health and brought him prematurely to the grave. He was not to be persuaded and fettered in this way; his conscience told him that it was quite lawful to labour on the Sabbath if circumstances required it, and he was evidently disposed, like Hillel, to set conduct above outward observances. But, unfortunately, while thus escaping from the Ritualists he presently allowed himself to be captured by the Mystics, who brought him under a still worse literal bondage. They made him a slave, not of ceremony, but of imaginary prediction; he was just as much subject to what had been written as an actor who performs his part on the stage; he was required to do such and such things, however unreasonable, inopportune, or against the dictates of conscience, in order that the Scripture might be fulfilled. His teachers did not urge him to keep noble examples always in sight, and thus establish a moral relationship with eminent men who had lived in the past; they were only anxious that between his words and acts and those of ancient Israelites there should be a mystic relationship. He was therefore instructed to ride into Jerusalem mounted on a young ass, and submit to be crucified precisely at the time of the offering of the Paschal Lamb.

Jesus was crucified in accordance with the arrangement of the Arimathæan and other esoteric partisans simply as Messiah. But it was inevitable that the supernatural character which they contrived to give him by illusory appearances should lead in a little while to Messiah-worship and a new theology. When he was supposed to have risen from the dead and ascended into Heaven there was gradually extended among the growing community of disciples a belief in his Divine attributes. They searched the Scriptures diligently and found what they wished to discover—found that he was everywhere portrayed and prefigured in a wonderful manner from the beginning of Genesis to the end of Malachi. When they thus assured themselves that his coming was spoken of by the patriarchs and hinted at even from the time of the Creation, the notion of his pre-existence naturally arose; it was believed that one who had been an object of great interest from the beginning of the world must be something more than man, must be really the companion of the Eternal. Several mystic theories were therefore propounded in reference to the risen Christ; some were disposed to class him with the angels, others thought he was probably the Platonic Logos, or Divine Creative Word, and the majority were at length disposed to believe that he was the " Son of God begotten of his Father before all worlds." As this doctrine got to be established in the Church, his sacrificial death at Calvary was rendered more mysterious, and at the same time it became less than ever reconcilable with a belief in Divine justice.

In the opinion of good Jews it was a monstrous wrong, an outrageous cruelty for a man to sacrifice his son as was done by some of their heathen neighbours. If they had remonstrated with the Syrians and others in reference to the shocking custom, the latter would undoubtedly have answered that they only did it under a pressing necessity to avert worse consequences. They loved their children and were grieved to part with them, but were fully convinced that unless they sacrificed a few at a critical time to appease the wrath of Baal, he would presently destroy all. The Jews would not have admitted the force of such an argument because they did not believe in Baal, but they knew themselves that it made a great difference whether a cruel act was done optionally or from sheer necessity. In some of their protracted sieges starving women had occasionally devoured their own children to sustain life, when parent and offspring must otherwise have speedily perished together. The Jews, too, believed that a person in a state of subjection was bound to do any terrible thing that he was commanded to do, and could not be considered guilty in consequence as though he had acted from his own free choice. A soldier who, in obedience to orders, struck down his fellow-men on the battle-field, was not to be regarded as a murderer; a man who gave up his sons freely for the king's service was not to be reproached as a cruel parent who had needlessly turned out his children to perish. The story of Abraham's preparation to slay his son Isaac was evidently meant to show that the patriarch's conduct was right and proper under the circumstances, because he was in the position of a servant, and therefore compelled to do what he was told, however much against his own wishes. But if the story had said that he prepared to slay Isaac without being commanded to do so and entirely of his own free motion, there would have been no excuse for such a cruel resolve, and he would have been considered a monster of wickedness. The case, however, would have been far worse if Abraham, instead of proceeding to sacrifice his son solemnly and decently on an altar, had delivered him into the hands of his servants to mock, scourge, and crucify as the only condition of their receiving pardon for their numerous transgressions. Yet according to the Christian the ology this is just the way in which the Divine Father, with no terrible necessity behind him, treated the innocent Messiah in giving him up to wicked people to be tormented for the wickedness of mankind; there is no parallel to the monstrous legend in the wildest extravagances of heathendom.

The orthodox theology not only gives us an extremely low, barbarous conception of God, but it considerably reduces the moral stature of Jesus. He repeatedly applied to himself the designation "Son of Man," as Ezekiel and other Jewish prophets had done before him, but he never dreamt of setting up a claim to Divinity. The notion of a Divine being of infinite wisdom and benevolence artfully disguising himself and appearing on earth in human form so that the majority of people should mistake him for a man and treat him as such, is altogether preposterous. We are accustomed to say in these days that God communes spiritually with all men, having no need of a messenger. If, however, the cosmos were ordered differently, if, as people once supposed, God occupied a distant throne and ruled in the manner of a king, it is presumable that any Divine representative coming to our planet would at least be as well accredited as one who goes forth from this country as viceroy to a remote English dependency. We can conceive such a thing as a Son of God visiting our earth for a time to enlighten its inhabitants and promote their well-being. In that case he would know that very little good could be effected unless he were so completely distinguished from other people that everyone should instantly recognise his Divinity. He might come, for instance, marvellously suspended in the air, or might appear as a giant twenty feet high, or towering above men as an ordinary man rises above the stature of children. Distinguished in this way it would be possible for him to command at once universal respect as a teacher and legislator, and introduce such wise arrangements as would greatly ameliorate the condition of the whole human family. If he did nothing more than act as a supreme magistrate and organise a pure administration of justice so as not only to settle the disputes of individuals, but the sanguinary strife between rival communities, he would thus confer on mankind an incalculable amount of good.

It is made out that Jesus could have done all this and much more if he had pleased, only that he was desirous of appearing among men incognito. He is said to have spent the greater portion of his earthly sojourn at Nazareth, and to have passed himself off there with so much art as a mechanic that not the slightest suspicion was entertained among the neighbours of his being anything else. If we accept the popular theory of his Divinity, it would seem to have been with him a paramount object to keep up an illusory appearance and maintain at all costs his human disguise. He could have increased his stature to any extent if he had pleased to do so, but according to the Gospel of Peter he never attempted to exercise this power till he rose from the tomb in strict privacy, and then he suddenly towered to the heavens. He could have flown through the air when he liked as easily as a bird; knowing, however, that many eyes were upon him, he kept his feet carefully to the ground, and it was only when he took his final departure from earth that he happened to be seen by one or two people in the act of volitation. Even in the miracles of transmutation, healing, and exorcism which he is said to have wrought, he seems to have studied to keep strictly within the range of the marvellous performances which were exhibited by thaumaturgists of that period. Consequently everybody supposed that he was really a man and nothing more; if people could have only seen through his disguise and known that a Divine being of unlimited wisdom and power was moving about among them, they would have flocked together from all parts to hear his discourses, and would reverently have fallen at his feet.

A teacher deserves honour not according to his powers or talents or the amount of knowledge which he may possess, but according as he conscientiously exerts himself and does the best that he possibly can for the world's enlightenment. The strenuous efforts made by some men with comparatively little learning to impart what they know to others, are more to be esteemed than great abilities and splendid attainments which are turned to very little account. If it be allowed that Jesus was simply a Galilean peasant living among other peasants in an atmosphere of dense ignorance when a very prevalent belief existed that the end of the world was near, there is much in his enthusiastic exertions to rouse his countrymen and prepare for the impending crisis in human affairs which may well be entitled to admiration. And the illusions which led him to sacrifice his life were evidently forced on him by others and not evolved from his own mind, as some investigators have been disposed to believe. Probably many distinguished teachers of this age would acquit themselves less creditably than he did, if they could only be thrown back to the unenlightened times in which he lived, and placed in precisely the same circumstances. But his idolatrous followers have all along committed a great mistake in thinking to exhance his reputation by ascribing to him Divine attributes. For if he was really endowed with supernatural powers, if he knew all things and could do whatever he pleased, there is not a shadow of excuse for his failing to rule and beneficially influence not merely his own countrymen, but the entire world. To make out that he had unlimited resources as a teacher and yet did not care to utilise them, that he knew all that is known in the present century, and a great deal more, but had no inclination to impart it to others, is to immensely diminish his moral worth. Indeed, if it be granted that he was a Divine being who could have commanded universal attention and immensely accelerated human progress, what he did and submitted to be done to during his sojourn on earth, is no more entitled to respect than those idle interventions and miraculous freaks ascribed to the gods of the heathen mythology.

§ 5.—*Vicarious Atonement.*

The Rev. Dr. Herman Adler, the highest Jewish authority in this country, after referring in one of his published sermons to the mistranslation of Isaiah liii. 8 in the Christian Bible, which offers a false ground for the doctrine of Vicarious Atonement, and he thinks may have suggested it, proceeds to show that it is utterly inconsistent and irreconcilable with Divine justice.

"Every man," says the Chief Rabbi, "is accountable for his own actions and cannot release himself from his individual responsibility by the vicarious atonement of another, however great he may be. We have no mediator to save us from the effects of our guilt but our own sincere repentance. . . . This doctrine of individual responsibility is again and again insisted on in the Bible. It is clearly set forth in the 18th and 33rd chapters of Ezekiel. I will quote a few verses from them: 'The soul that sinneth it shall die.' 'The son shall not bear the iniquity of the father, neither shall the father bear the iniquity of the son.' And further on, 'I will judge you, O house of Israel, every one according to his ways.' These verses tell us that we are all responsible beings; no one can, no one need make expiation for our sins. We require nothing but our own repentance and the love and mercy of our God to obtain forgiveness and salvation.

"It has, however, been urged that the Bible shadows forth and typifies the doctrine of vicarious atonement in the law of sacrifices. . . . You will at once see that these arguments rest on an entirely false idea of the object and value of sacrifices. I have on a former occasion shown how the Bible teaches us that offerings were quite inefficacious unless accompanied by sincere repentance and devout contrition. When a man had been guilty of any trespass against his neighbour, when he had withheld what was entrusted to him, or taken something by violence, he was enjoined first to redress the wrong committed, and then to bring his trespass offering. The only value and efficacy of the offering consisted in this, that it proved the sacrificer to be repentant; it was an outward test and sign of his sincerity. It has been asserted that the atonement which the high-priest made on the great day for that purpose teaches that man can mediate between God and the sinner. But this assertion also rests on an error. Our sages teach us, 'for him who sins with the idea that the Day of Atonement will expiate his guilt, that day is of no avail' (Mishna, Joma, cviii. 9). The whole object of that Day is to impress on us the truth that we have no mediation to save us from our sins but our own sincere repentance.

"Let us now consider what would be the consequence of a vicarious atonement. The good man and the wicked would thereby be reduced to the same level. The righteous who erred, and the profligate who erred, would both alike receive the Divine grace, the former by his own merit, the latter by the merit of his mediator, and the whole end and purpose of our earthly life would be stultified. The probation to which we are now subjected would be of no avail. And if it were so, why should a man yield up his pleasures, his passions, his material interests, his self, to good works that may be dispensed with, to virtues that are unnecessary? Indeed, the theory of mediation, if carried to its extreme consequences, would be a monstrous reversal of the Divine scheme of man's creation and destiny. No: such cannot be the way of the Perfect Judge. The Pentateuch and the Prophets tell us most unequivocally that it is not, and reason leads to the same conclusion" ("Sabbath Readings," iv. 27—Sermon iii.).

Some men are much better than the crooked theological doctrines to which they persistently cling, and they naturally feel disposed to embellish those doctrines, and present them to the world in a more favourable light. Mr. Gladstone, in a recent apologetic article on the Atonement, says: "The great sacrifice of Calvary does not undermine or enfeeble, but illuminates and sustains the moral law." In reality this superstition of the primitive Church has precisely the same effect on people's minds as that of the older sacrifices. If a few noble characters continue to believe in the mysterious doctrine of the Cross without being apparently less virtuous and amiable for so doing, it will be found to have a decidedly prejudicial influence on the conduct of others. Plenty of people may be met with at the present day who lead discreditable lives, and cannot be stirred to amendment, because they think that a strict discharge of duty is not at all incumbent on them, that mere virtue is of very little worth, that the one essential thing is an unbounded trust in the merits of Christ. In some instances they even take a sort of pride in being poor believing sinners, and they look with contempt on those who justify themselves by honourable conduct, being under the impression that reliance on probity will sink such mistaken souls to perdition, while their own faith in the sacrificial blood shed for human redemption will carry them straight to Paradise.

Rude, ignorant, and immoral people generally have a profound disbelief in virtue, and a desire to obtain happiness by sheer good fortune. They care not for justice, and are constantly seeking after favour of some kind or other, yet the experienced and wise know that favour, even if secured, is not simply a doubtful advantage to its recipients, but a positive curse. Let the father of a family show especial indulgence towards one son—yield to his selfish entreaties, lighten his labours, overlook his transgressions, invariably side with him in all the strife which he has with his brethren—and how will such treatment affect his character and future welfare? It cannot fail to make him a proud, idle, conceited quarrelsome youth, whom everybody will hate and despise; and, instead or eventually prospering and becoming the foremost member of the family, he will, in all probability, end his days as a criminal or a vagabond. Let a magistrate, a prince, or any other ruler, treat with like partiality a certain portion of his subject people, that is, humour their vicious propensities, confer on them honours and privileges which they have not fairly earned, permit them to break the laws with impunity, and it will be found that they are not, in the end, wiser, better, and more prosperous for such treatment, but just the reverse. The favours heaped on them will only lead them to have too good an opinion of themselves, and they will, therefore, act in such a rash and inconsiderate manner, and provoke so much hostility as to render confusion and disaster at length inevitable. If we can suppose the Ruler of the Universe departing from true equity to humour certain individuals or communities by occasionally interrupting the course of nature to save them from the consequences of their folly and neglect, it would produce precisely the same kind of moral injury as the favours conferred by any human government. Those who obtained the Divine indulgences would be exempted from much wholesome discipline, would be encouraged to live idly, carelessly, and extravagantly, and so would be found, after all the partiality shown them, to be less wise and happy than the rest of mankind.

If we do wrong, let us by all means be punished for that wrong and so we shall presently learn to do right; it cannot possibly be for our advantage to go on committing all kinds of foolish and wicked acts without correction. Still less can it conduce to our permanent benefit to entertain the belief in the world being so governed that, while we have to suffer for the faults of our remote ancestors, we may still escape the pains that our own transgressions deserve, because an entirely innocent person is punished in our stead. Mr. Gladstone, writing in defence of this outrageous doctrine, says:—

"It is not by any innovation, so to speak, in his scheme of government that the Almighty brings about this great and glorious result. What is here enacted on a gigantic scale in the kingdom of grace, only repeats a phenomenon with which we are all familiar in the natural and social order of the world, where the good at the expense of pain endured by them procure benefits for the unworthy. The Christian atonement is, indeed, transcendent in character, and cannot receive from ordinary sources any entirely adequate illustration, but yet the essential and root of this matter lies in the idea of good vicariously conveyed. And this is an operation appertaining to the whole order of human things, so that besides being agreeable to justice and to love, it is also sustained by analogies lying outside the Christian system, and indeed the whole order of revelation."

But any sacrificial suffering on the part of the

innocent that the guilty may go scot free, whether in accordance with heathen or with Christian teaching, is not really "agreeable to justice," and the "analogies" here presented to us are entirely false and misleading. In the natural and social order of the world, benevolent people will be found constantly labouring and taking much trouble to assist the worthy, but they do not in general present themselves as victims and invite the infliction of murderous cruelty with the view to procure benefits for the unworthy. If a man works hard to support his wife and children and comes home every evening with aching limbs, it will be acknowledged that he has thus far worthily discharged his parental duty. If he sustains severe bodily injuries in endeavouring to save his neighbours from fire or flood, or in defending them from lawless aggression, such heroic suffering will not fail to procure for him much sympathy and the lasting esteem of his countrymen. On the other hand, one who puts himself and his household on short commons in order to discharge the liabilities of some reckless spendthrift will be thought to act with the greatest folly. And if he were to intercede strongly in behalf of a garroter who had been arrested and sentenced to flogging, and offer to receive the punishment in his stead, he would probably be considered out of his mind. Rational suffering for a good purpose, cannot be deemed analogous to vicarious atonements, or legitimately appealed to as a justification for the severe self-tortures which ascetics submitted to in a barbarous and superstitious age.

CHAPTER II.

THE PLAIN PASSION-DRAMA.

§ 1.—*Nazarene Asceticism.*

IN the preceding chapter we have endeavoured to make the crucifixion of Jesus intelligible as a mystic immolation planned and carried out by his own esoteric partisans, of whom the most influential was, probably, Joseph of Arimathæa. They would have committed a distinct breach of the law by sacrificing him openly, even if his willingness to die in that way had been well known and publicly declared. Besides, such an outrageous proceeding would have savoured of heathenism, would have been offensive to all parties, and must necessarily have brought speedy ruin to their cause. They had good reasons, therefore, for giving his sacrificial death an appearance of martyrdom so as to free themselves from all reproach in connection with it, and at the same time cast discredit on the Jewish authorities. The study of those portions of Isaiah which speak of the oppression of Israel in a state of exile had led them to believe that there was thus foreshown the suffering of the Messiah at the hands of his enemies. It was necessary, according to their view, that he should not only die as a sacrifice, but be subjected in addition to terrible ill-treatment and wrong, in order that what the Scripture said concerning him should be properly fulfilled. And if such injustice as captive Israel experienced from the conquering Chaldeans did not actually fall upon him, there must at least be a semblance of it exhibited.

Previous to the Babylonian exile, and even long

afterwards, the best Jewish teachers maintained that Divine justice was established on earth; they believed that people were dealt with on the whole equitably in the present state of existence. It was declared that though a good man might suffer wrong for a while, or experience much trouble, and a bad man might enjoy temporary prosperity, each would be requited in the end according to his deserts. "I have been young and now am old, yet have I not seen the righteous forsaken nor his seed begging bread. . . . . I have seen the wicked in great power, and spreading himself like a green bay-tree, yet he passed away, and lo he was not." (Psalm xxxvii. 25-35). The story of the patriarch Joseph is intended to show that Divine justice in the course of a few years corrects human injustice. The Book of Job presents a striking picture of a good man patiently enduring a succession of adversities which bring him to the verge of death, yet recovering himself and becoming more prosperous than ever at last. Those who held these views, and were satisfied with the conditions of their earthly existence, might still believe in a future life, but they had no idea of its being expressly designed for the correction of whatever ills and wrongs are now permissible.

In the course of time, however, there arose another school of religious teachers who, not being satisfied with the requital which human conduct now receives, believed that Divine justice could only make things straight by rewards and punishments which would be administered hereafter. They were generally pious, meditative men, without much industrial energy, and they relied more on prayer than on labour for procuring themselves the means of subsistence. Consequently, with all their devotions and persevering practice of saintship, they only reaped the reward of the slothful, and often fell into a condition of abject poverty. On the other hand, they beheld some of their more energetic neighbours, whom they thought ungodly, prospering from year to year and surrounded by the comforts and enjoyments of life. This was altogether wrong in their estimation, and would have to be corrected in another state of existence. The poor saint would be compensated for his present ill-fortune by unbounded prosperity in the future world, and the rich people who despised him would be subjected in turn to perpetual humiliation and shame.

Many Jews were not able to reconcile the long succession of adversities which they experienced as a nation with the establishment of Divine justice on earth. They thought that their strict Sabbath-keeping and freedom from the pollution of images ought to have made them the foremost people in the world, yet they saw Gentile communities, who despised all their regulations, in a more prosperous condition than themselves. "Are they then of Babylon better than they of Sion? Or is there any other people that knoweth thee besides Israel? Or what generation hath so believed thy covenants as Jacob? And yet their reward appeareth not, and their labour hath no fruit; for I have gone here and there through the heathen, and I see that they flow in wealth, and think not on thy commandments" (2 Esdras iv. 31-33). The mystery was at length solved to the satisfaction of some; it got to be believed in time that Israel was a righteous saint-nation despised and ill-treated by wicked Gentiles, and that, like each individual saint, it would eventually in a day of retribution rise from the dust and be exalted in Heaven, and behold its oppressors humiliated. The end of the world was supposed to be near when the heathen nations would perish entirely, and the kingdom of the twelve tribes, instead of being restored on earth, would be established in Heaven everlastingly (Dan. ii. 44; xii. 2-3).

As Palestine fell completely under Roman rule, and there seemed little probability of national independence being recovered by a further resort to force, those Jews who believed in the predictions of "Daniel" and "Enoch," directed their hopes of a brighter future more and more to the prospective Kingdom of Heaven. It was often asked, especially by men depressed with trouble and adversity, when that glorious dominion of the saints would be established, and what signs would appear that people might prepare for its coming? But the greatest anxiety was felt to know who would be considered worthy to enter its gates and enjoy everlasting felicity, and who would be rigorously excluded. Some thought that it was simply necessary to lead a virtuous life in order to gain hereafter admission to the realms of bliss. Others entertained the opinion that there would be no room provided for any who had been prosperous on earth, even though they had kept strictly the precepts of the Law, and that the best title to admission would be the suffering of much wrong, and the experience of great misery and poverty. Most people in good circumstances, on being told that their enjoyments were brief, and that they would have to endure eventually endless woe by way of requital, entirely disbelieved what was said by those who presumed to admonish them. But some were led to consider the predictions of doom which they heard from one and another well-founded, and were brought in consequence to completely revolutionise their habits of life. If fortunes were to be reversed at the great Judgment they began to think it wise to have their evil lot first, so as to become entitled at length to an endless period of blissful compensation. Instead of seeking for wealth, therefore, and continually adding to their comforts, they raced in an opposite direction and strove to outdo each other in poverty and misery, after the manner of the world-renouncing saints. The most profitable course that people could take in their estimation was to live a life of extreme wretchedness, and thus look forward with confidence to being gloriously requited by a corresponding elevation in Paradise.

Some of the Pharisees not only renounced wealth and worldly pleasures, but practised long abstinence and very severe penances with the view to qualify themselves for admission to the Kingdom of Heaven. The Essenes, with the same object before them, lived in strict celibacy, and delivered themselves from the reproach of heaping up riches by establishing a communistic brotherhood. The Nazarenes were a kindred sect of speculative saints who, in order to prepare more effectively for the promised heavenly kingdom, went so far as to organise its government. There were rich people among them who retained their wealth for a time and so rendered the community very important services, but they were not qualified for holding high office. It was thought that those who would be called to sit on thrones hereafter, and rule the twelve tribes, must necessarily be men of the poorest and humblest condition. Jesus and his disciples, being Galilean peasants, might reasonably aspire to an elevation in the future world such as would never be granted to any who were found in a higher and more honourable station on earth. Legend even said that he was born in a stable and cradled in a manger to make his low estate more strikingly manifest as a proof of his entire fitness to rule the saints in the Kingdom of Heaven.

The reversal of human fortunes at the coming Judgment was clearly the fundamental doctrine insisted on in the teaching of Jesus. " Woe unto you that are rich, for ye have received your reward." " Whosoever exalteth himself shall be abased, and he that humbleth himself shall be exalted." "Thou in thy lifetime receivedst good things and likewise Lazarus evil things, but now he is comforted and thou art tormented" (Luke vi. 24; xiv. 11; xvi. 25). Keeping of the commandments or leading a virtuous life would avail nothing to insure future felicity for those who were enjoying present abundance (Matt. xix. 23, 24). The prosperous man, instead of waiting like Job for a series of calamities to befall him, was to voluntarily part with all his possessions and court adversity and impoverishment. One who subsisted in comfort on the fruits of skilled labour was to abandon his occupation, distribute his goods, and wander forth in the condition of a mendicant, without having any place where to lay his head. If he enjoyed good health he was to mortify his flesh by much fasting, by miserable lodging, and by travelling barefoot and scantily clothed, exposed to all the roughness of the roads and the weather's inclemency. Those who would know from observation what the religious asceticism practised both by Nazarenes and Pharisees was like, will find examples of it at the present day in India rather than in England.

"The spirit of the gospel is a holy eagerness of suffering," says Massillon, and this spirit is now very little understood by Protestant communities engaged in the race for wealth and worldly enjoyment. We hear it now and then said of some person, that he has got a heavy cross to bear, which means simply that he has got a trouble of some kind to vex him from which he would gladly be released. But the early Christians longed to bear a cross in reality, believing that no better fortune could possibly await them than that of being stoned, scourged, imprisoned, tortured, and finally led forth and crucified. In their ardent desire to suffer with the view to being amply recompensed they valued most of all any pain that was inflicted on them by opponents so that it could be accounted persecution. " Blessed are ye when men shall revile you and persecute you . . . Whosoever shall smite thee on thy right cheek turn to him the other also. And if any man will sue thee at the law and take away thy coat, let him have thy cloak also. And whosoever shall compel thee to go a mile go with him twain " (Matt. v. 11., 39-41). But if they lived in quiet times, and it was not easy to provoke persecution, they were expected to afflict themselves by abstaining from food, sacrificing their virility, or some other act of voluntary suffering. Only it was considered good policy to disguise penances and present an appearance of being undevout and worldly so as to get no praise from men and secure the greater compensation in Heaven. " When thou fastest anoint thy head and wash thy face that thou appear not unto men to fast, but unto thy Father, which is in secret, and thy Father which seeth in secret shall reward thee openly " (Matt. vi. 17, 18).

Many of the early ascetic Christians acted strictly in accordance with the Gospel precepts. The celebrated Origen lived an austere life, and after failing to obtain the crown of martyrdom, as his father had done, made himself a eunuch for the Kingdom of Heaven's sake. We are told of St. Felix: " He never looked any woman in the face. He walked always barefoot even without sandals. . . . . When he ate alone and thought no one saw him, he practised incredible austerities; but when he dined in company with others he endeavoured ordinarily to shun any singularity that could be taken notice of. He disguised his mortifications under various pretences, and excused his going without sandals, saying he walked more easily without them; but he suppressed the inconveniences which he felt in that mortification. It was his study to conceal from others as much as possible all heavenly favours, and to avoid whatever might give them a good opinion of him" ("Lives of the Saints").

When there was no prospect of suffering from persecution, all the greater need was felt of resorting to some kind of penance. One of the most famous of self-torturing Christians was St. Simeon Stylites. On hearing the beatitudes read one day when a mere youth, "Blessed are they that mourn," &c., he entreated an old man to tell him the meaning of these words, and asked how the promised happiness was to be obtained. He was told that continual prayer, watching, fasting, weeping, humiliation, and patient suffering of persecutions were pointed out in these texts as the true road to happiness. He soon after entered a monastery, and while the monks there were accustomed to eat but once a day, he so far exceeded their rule of abstinence as to take but one meal a weak. Observing a disused well-rope made of twisted palm leaves, he resolved to make it serve as an instrument of penance, and therefore bound it about his naked body, where it remained unknown to the rest of the community till it had worn into the flesh and was discovered at length by the stench proceeding from the wound. For three successive days his clothes which clung to it had to be moistened with liquids to disengage them, and the incisions made in cutting the rope from his body were attended with such anguish that he lay for some time almost dead. He soon after withdrew to a hermitage at the foot of Mount Thelanissa, where he was accustomed to pass the whole forty days of Lent in total abstinence. As many people visited his retreat and flocked about to receive his blessing, he built a stone enclosure to be delivered from their interruptions, but had no roof to protect him from the inclemency of the weather. He next erected a pillar six cubits high, and on it dwelt four years; on a second, twelve cubits high, he lived three years; on a third, twenty-two cubits high, ten years; and on a fourth, forty cubits high, built for him by the people, he spent the last twenty years of his life. He exercised at one time almost as much power as a mediæval pope; princes and bishops bowed reverently before him and respected his word as though it were a voice from Heaven. Several other Eastern saints followed his example, yet without being able to achieve a corresponding amount of success. Dr. Schaff, the Protestant historian, writing of the numerous Christians who adopted a monastic or a solitary life in the fourth century, says: "Monasticism also afforded a compensation for martyrdom which ceased with the Christianisation of the State, and thus gave place to a voluntary martyrdom, a gradual self-destruction, a sort of religious suicide. In the burning deserts and awful caverns of Syria and Egypt, amidst the pains of self-torture, the mortification of natural desires, and relentless battles with hellish monsters, the ascetics now sought to win the crown of heavenly glory which their predecessors in the times of persecution had more quickly and easily gained by a bloody death" ("History of the Christian Church," Vol. II. p. 155).

As the practice of austerities in some form or other was thus thought indispensable for the attainment of Heaven when the storm of persecution ceased, so it was considered equally necessary in the period of calm before hostility was encountered. We are told that Jesus wandered into a wilderness where he disputed with the Devil, and afflicted himself with long fasting, as was afterwards done by St. Antony and other anchorites who claimed to be his genuine disciples. He probably had recourse to various self-mortifications which were not recorded, as it was his general policy to disguise acts of asceticism lest he should thereby attract notice and obtain the praise of men so as to diminish the recompense awaiting him in Paradise. His final great ordeal of suffering on the cross, like that of St. Simeon on the pillar, was of such a nature that it could not be carried out entirely by himself, and a certain amount of publicity was unavoidable.

§ 2.—*Assisted Penances.*

It is well known that crucifixion, besides being a cruel punishment in ancient times, has also been resorted to as a penance, just as people have now and then voluntarily pilloried themselves to atone for some past offence. Considering the wonderful attraction that this form of suffering has for ascetic minds, it probably would have been frequently adopted in the Christian Church if it had only been permissible. In the course of time it got to be invested with so much sanctity that it was prohibited by the Emperor Constantine as a punishment, and an ordinary Christian was supposed to be wholly unworthy of the honour of such treatment as a penance. Moreover, it could not be accomplished without assistance, so that those who were ambitious of suffering as Christ did, generally had to be contented with inflicting on themselves the *stigmata*, or five crucifixion wounds. But in the reign of Louis XV., the French Convulsionaries pondered a good deal over the text, " He that taketh not his cross and followeth after me is not worthy of me " (Matt. x. 38), and so determined were they to act up to this declaration of the master, as they understood it, that they managed to crucify one another. Some of these ascetics were not satisfied with being nailed up once, they underwent the terrible ordeal several times, and remained on the cross from two to three hours without flinching.

Evidently an assisted penance is in its moral aspect very much like a courted martyrdom. In the former case a person suffers voluntarily with the help of his friends, while in the latter he provokes from those who oppose or dispute with him pains which are supposed to be conducive to his welfare. The English Government has of late years done much to suppress assisted penances in India, not regarding them as criminal acts, but as barbarous exhibitions calculated to produce an unwholesome effect on the public mind. If some of the Convulsionaries had died when painfully suspended on the cross, their companions who nailed them up would have been blamed undoubtedly, but they could not be charged with murder, because they had no evil intent, and simply studied the gratification of the sufferers' wishes. So among the early Christians who died as martyrs there were some not in the least aggrieved, but extremely obliged by the pains inflicted on them, and those who deprived them of life under such circumstances, if culpable, were not really criminal. One of the companions of Cyprian writes : " Though we have not yet shed our blood, but are prepared to shed it, no one may think this postponement clemency, for it injures us, it interposes a hindrance to our glory ; it puts off Heaven." Cyprian himself was so pleased at the prospect of suffering martyrdom that he bequeathed twenty pieces of gold to the executioner who struck off his head. The Donatists went so far as to use actual violence and resolve on taking the Kingdom of Heaven by force (Matt. xi. 12). They rudely disturbed Pagan festivals and profaned some of the temples in order to exasperate the worshippers and provoke them to a furious retaliation. Some forced their way into the courts of justice and insulted the magistrates in the hope of being ordered to immediate execution. Others impeded the traffic on public roads, and were not content till they were struck down by angry travellers and beaten severely or actually trampled to death.

It was to them a matter of comparative indifference under what form of violence they suffered so long as they could assure themselves of thus attaining to the glory of martyrdom.

Jesus, as well as his followers, calculated on profitable suffering either in the way of martyrdom or penance, and living as he did in peaceful times, it was only by the latter method that it was possible for him to obtain the desired amount of affliction. In the Nazarene belief the Kingdom of Heaven was prepared solely as a place of compensation for those who were treated badly or had a miserable existence on earth. The saints who went there were expected to be poor sufferers, victims of oppression and wrong, and the Messiah who reigned over them must necessarily endure the greatest abasement of all. According to the law of reversal, it was only the most impoverished and downtrodden members of the community that could have the highest places in Paradise. It was believed that Isaiah's personification of Israel in a miserable condition of exile as one suffering undeserved punishment, "a man of sorrows and acquainted with grief," pointed prophetically to the Messiah; therefore no-one could have any claim to be the promised redeemer unless he was in an impoverished condition and subjected at the same time to insult and ill-usage. How then could Jesus go into training and sufficiently qualify himself to win the respect and obtain the loyal support of that portion of his countrymen who believed in a suffering Messiah? It was easy enough to part with what little property he had and become extremely poor, but by no means easy for one who led an innocent life in quiet times to provoke the requisite amount of bad treatment. He could hardly have committed a greater offence than that of speaking his mind plainly to hot-tempered people, whereby he would have incurred at the utmost an occasional slap in the face. Any more serious and cruel suffering that he might have considered it necessary to undergo must have been some form of penance at the hands of those who desired to advance his interests; it could not possibly have been inflicted as a punishment by his religious opponents.

Not only was the crucifixion of Jesus, considered as a punishment, frightfully disproportionate to any offence that he could have possibly committed, but it was aggravated by mockery and insult. People sentenced to death have occasionally been insulted when brought to execution, where they have been heartless murderers or proud, sanguinary tyrants, so as to provoke a feeling in the minds of spectators that the cruelty which they inflicted on others had now at length come home to themselves. No such fierce mockery could have been excited in the human breast by the sufferings of Jesus; he had never been in a lordly position that people could exult over his fall; he had killed no one, defrauded no one, neither had he passed sentence on a single individual, or exercised any kind of government oppression. It was well known that he was a poor homeless wanderer who had fared miserably enough, and to see a man in that beggared condition taken and cruelly tormented must have moved his stoutest religious opponents to commiseration. The chief priests could not possibly have been so inhuman and forgetful of their dignity as to gloat over the execution of the poor Galilean teacher, and even revile him in his death agony. Dramatic representation could very well make them appear to do so, but supposing them to have been present in reality, such a shameful exhibition of malevolence on their part would imply that they were not only persons of low brutalised disposition, but downright savages.

On the other hand, if it be admitted that the Crucifixion was contrived and carried out by the partisans of Jesus as a Messianic sacrifice and penance, we have not only explained the absence of all opposition to it on the part of the spectators, but the outrageous proceedings described by the Evangelists are perfectly intelligible, and what might be expected to occur. According to the law of reversal, then firmly believed by the Nazarenes, it was necessary that the Messiah should have the greatest possible abasement on earth or he could not be sufficiently exalted in Heaven. His religious opponents would never have thought him so bad a character that he deserved to be insulted, beaten, buffeted, crowned with thorns, and finally crucified between two thieves, but such treatment is just what would be suggested by the genius of asceticism as especially desirable in consideration of his future advancement. To afflict him and make him an object of scorn and derision, was in Nazarene estimation to fufil Scripture in his behalf and give him a sure title to everlasting honour. His partisans looked beyond the present pains which he endured, and contemplated the felicity and glory which they expected him to obtain as a recompense when promoted to the highest place in the Kingdom of Heaven.

It seems a hard thing for people to inflict pain on those whom they love and hold in high esteem, but it is done even now in the case of patients who are subjected to severe surgical treatment which is expected to conduce to their permanent benefit. If affectionate relatives have not the heart to wound a brother or sister themselves, in such circumstances they will readily pay someone else to do it for them. It is the same in the case of assisted penances; the Convulsionaries had nerve enough to crucify beloved members of the fraternity with their own hands. At Berne, in 1507, the Dominicans did not go so far as to crucify their brother Jetzer, but they stamped on him with a sharp nail the five crucifixion wounds and stretched him crosswise on an altar exposed to the view of the superstitious multitude. Their aim was not simply to exalt the merits of Jetzer as a saint and give him a claim to great future glory; they sought as well to advance the immediate interests of their Order and throw discredit on their rivals the Franciscans. Their stratagem succeeded well for a time, but was at length exposed; and, as usually happens when such bold designs break down, they brought on themselves shame and confusion. The Nazarenes may have been influenced by purer motives and loftier aims than these unfortunate Dominicans, who fifteen hundred years afterwards professed to tread in their footsteps; but they at least resembled them in hoping to gain Heaven by much suffering. They were also no less determined by all possible means to overthrow the claims of their religious rivals, and they were equally ready and more successful in contriving dramatic apparitions for convincing the credulous that they were favoured with the visits of celestial messengers.

§ 3.—*Transfiguration and Trial.*

It has been shown that the crucifixion of Jesus, viewed as a Messianic penance, was, according to the prevalent belief of those times, a well-contrived means to an end, a necessary abasement on earth to earn as compensation a future supremacy in Heaven. We will now consider again the further purpose which it served as a dramatic spectacle for influencing opinion and attracting to the Nazarene movement popular sympathy. Dramatic action, so disguised that it passed for natural action, was unquestionably a great exciting power in the primitive Church, and there is good reason to believe that it produced some of the miraculous scenes presented to us by the Evangelists, which are now often explained as mythical. Luke, or the author of Acts, tells us of Ananias and Sapphira being struck dead for not making a strictly accurate statement of what they had realised by the sale of their property. Some Christian scholars are inclined to consider this a fiction, because, as generally understood, it amounts, as they say, to a charge of deliberate murder against Peter. It looks as if he had seized on a frivolou-excuse to kill the man and his wife mysteriously that the Church might be relieved from their further support and appropriate the whole of their possessions. Moreover, it cannot be supposed that Peter would punish with so much severity unveracious speaking in newly-converted people when he had recently erred in this respect himself, notwithstanding his long discipleship. But the narrative is not one likely to have been invented, and if it be allowed that the writer may be here reporting a dramatic scene, the conduct of the chief Apostle at once assumes a different complexion. It is not unreasonable to suppose that Ananias and Sapphira were actors in a masked drama, and that their penal deaths were feigned for the purpose of strongly impressing converts and deterring them from understating the amount of their possessions, which some of them might naturally be expected to do on joining the communistic brotherhood. In such case the worst that can be said of Peter is that he had a very rude and objectionable method of inculcating truthfulness, though not much unlike the expedients occasionally resorted to in the mediæval Church for frightening simple people from an immoral course.

In the story of the Transfiguration we have a miracle of an exactly opposite character to that reported in the fifth chapter of Acts. Instead of two people being struck dead, it is made to appear that Moses and Elias, who had been dead for a long time, were brought back to life. The great difficulty which confronts us here is not the miracle of these two eminent prophets reappearing in the land of Israel, but their strange and inconsistent behaviour after so coming back among their countrymen. During his former lifetime Moses ruled all Israel; he gave laws to a united people and established a permanent governing council of seventy elders who were expected to continue faithfully his judicial work. After having been now dead for several hundred years, he must have witnessed on his return to life some astonishing changes which had taken place among his countrymen. Instead of being a united community as he had left them, they were broken up into a number of discordant sects having different views of the nation's future and continually disputing about the right interpretation of the Law. The fierce strife of factions had weakened them and brought them under a foreign yoke, and some now looked for the restoration of their national independence, whilst others hoped for a happy future in the establishment of a Kingdom of Heaven. At Jerusalem the council of seventy elders still existed, but its judgment in matters of doctrine and discipline was not universally respected, while Jesus had even considered it advisable to organize a rival seventy. Here, then, was an opportunity for Moses to resume his judicial position and restore peace and harmony to the distracted nation, for however much the people were divided they all held him in very great honour, and were anxious to follow his teaching so far as they understood it and in every way submit to his authority. He could have told them at once what he really taught long ago, and what had since been imputed to him by others; he could have said what importance he attached to the prophetic visions of "Daniel" and "Enoch" in reference to the coming end of the world, and what opinion he had of Mysticism, Diabolism, Asceticism, Communism, and other imported notions which were greatly exciting the Jewish population. He might have settled promptly hundreds of perplexing questions; might have reconstructed and reformed the Sanhedrin if such a measure had been needed; and, calling together the heads of the various sects, might have so enlightened them concerning their differences as to allay all bitterness and bring them into friendly agreement. Indeed, his reappearance alone should have been sufficient to terminate for ever the old dispute between Sadducees and Pharisees. Yet, strange to say, this universally-respected judge of Israel, whose word was still law throughout the length and breadth of the land, instead of speaking openly to all parties according to his wont, simply favoured one sect with his presence at an obscure place in Galilee, and for anything that he did in the way of reconciling his divided countrymen and getting them to walk harmoniously together in the path of rectitude, he might as well have been an image of stone.

Assuming the Moses of the Transfiguration scene to be the real Moses who had been accustomed to speak authoritatively to all Israel and settle all disputes, anything more capricious than his avoiding the Sanhedrin and proceeding secretly to Galilee to commune only with a new sect can scarcely be imagined; he would thus completely stultify his former course as the national leader. But if we look at the scene in another light, if we take it to be a dramatic representation of Moses accompanied by Elias, it indicates that some of the partisans of Jesus had considerable ingenuity and resource in getting up appearances to serve as vouchers of his Messianic mission. It had been said by orthodox Jews that the chief priests and rulers were the true ministers of God, deriving their authority straight from Moses, and that this Nazarene leader in opposing them was an agent of Satan, even if he performed some good works (Matt. ix. 34; xii. 24). A similar charge has been levelled against the leaders of many new sects, which have revolted or seceded from established churches, and it is very natural that they should be branded in this way wherever the superstition of Diabolism exists. It is natural, too, that such a charge should give great offence to earnest, enthusiastic religious teachers, acting conscientiously and believing themselves Divinely guided, although in opposition to ecclesiastical authorities. A prophet has generally been able to match the pretensions of priests by claiming to receive a direct message from Heaven, and though he has no temple, it is possible to go to a mountain with a few trusty friends and extemporise as vouchers of his inspiration very impressive appearances. Some of the more intelligent Nazarenes, when they heard Jesus denounced as an emissary of Satan, were doubtless provoked to devise some strong argumentative method by which they might refute the calumny and even turn the tables on the calumniators. Certainly the Transfiguration scene was well calculated to produce a powerful impression on the simple disciples who were selected to witness it, and convince them that Jesus was supported by the greatest prophets of past times, and had, like them, received his authority from God. And if we now follow him from the Galilean mountain to Jerusalem and read with discernment the reports of his trial and crucifixion, we shall find good reasons for believing that these were also dramatic scenes equally well calculated to discredit the chief priests and rulers and make them appear iniquitous men under the direction of Satan.

Prophets who have been reared in humble circumstances, without any experience of government affairs, are not likely to sympathise with those who hold a ruling position and are responsible for maintaining order in a community. It is quite to be expected that all invested with regal power, or engaged in the administration of justice, should in their eyes seem alike heartless oppressors. Moreover, in the opinion of the Nazarenes, the judgment of misdeeds was to be entirely suspended on earth, and all charges of guilt were to stand over for the coming great Day of Assize. We cannot learn that Jesus ever cultivated friendly relations with men who acted as magistrates, and there is little doubt that, in common with the rest of his sect, he cordially hated the Jewish authorities. In modern times the intense hostility felt towards a national government by persons of ardent and visionary mind generally finds expression in the newspaper press. All eminent statesmen are fiercely assailed—in the satirical journals are outrageously caricatured, being often represented as rascally swindlers, and at other times as downright idiots. When Christianity was first preached there was no such effective means of lampooning rulers and holding them up to popular contempt; caricatures were occasionally drawn at roadsides and other places, but this could not be practised among the Jews. No one would have dared to daub on the walls of Jerusalem such rough satirical sketches as were seen in Gentile cities. Jesus called Herod Antipas a fox, and the Scribes and Pharisees serpents, yet neither he nor any other Jew would have presumed to depict men with bodies of beasts as was done in countries where painting was permissible. It is evident that a party influenced by strong adverse feelings against men in authority, yet unable to draw the human figure, or a distortion of it—from being under the prohibition of the Mosaic law, would be all the more likely to resort to dramatic action for the purpose of caricature.

We are told that Jesus, after conferring with the

two mysterious persons who represented Moses and Elias respecting the tragic close of his career, and charging the disciples to keep the matter secret for a time, went with them direct to Jerusalem for the express purpose of being there crucified, and so fulfilling Scripture as the suffering Messiah. All his movements are of a dramatic character, and seem to have been arranged by a Nazarene confederacy with whom he had secret intercourse. He was instructed to make his public entry into Jerusalem on a young ass, to accord with a passage of Zechariah ix. 9, which is supposed to refer to the humble condition of Zerubbabel when he came up from Chaldea with the restored captives to rebuild the city walls. He accordingly sent two of his disciples in advance, telling them that at a certain place they would find a colt tied, which the keepers would deliver into their hands. The disciples would be sure to consider the success of their enterprise a very satisfactory evidence that their master was gifted with foreknowledge and favoured with Divine assistance. Those who saluted Jesus with palm-branches and hosannas were merely servants of the confederacy, acting in accordance with their instructions. Again, on the day of unleavened bread, Peter and John—probably the same two disciples that procured the colt—were sent into the city to engage a room for the Passover. They were told that on entering the city a person would meet them bearing a pitcher of water, whom they were directed to follow home and say to the occupant of the house, "The master saith unto thee, Where is the guest chamber where I shall eat the passover with my disciples?" (Luke xxii. 11). Peter and John went into the city accordingly, and met a person as Jesus had foreshown, and made the preparations which he had directed. The house probably belonged to Joseph of Arimathæa, or some other influential Nazarene, and the whole business of its hire was a dramatic arrangement, although the simple disciples would readily believe that their proceedings were wonderfully correlated in accordance with supernatural design.

Soon after his first arrival in the city Jesus acted in much the same way that many Christians of the second century did when they sought to provoke persecution and martyrdom. He visited the Temple court and created a disturbance, for which it would have been quite lawful to imprison him for a time, or subject him to some other moderate punishment; but nothing of that kind seems to have resulted. At the Passover season religious zealots flocked into the city from every quarter, and great liberties were permitted them so long as they abstained from open rioting or insurrection. The Temple magistracy, acting in concert with the procurator, were not likely to be more alarmed or exasperated at the violent behaviour of Jesus than they were at the irregularities of other excited pilgrims who visited the city at the time of festivals. They might naturally suppose that in a few days he would return to his own province, and that nothing more would be heard of him, as it usually happened with such demonstrative enthusiasts. At any rate no attempt seems to have been made to check his disorderly proceedings in the Temple court and place him in confinement for a short period, when such repression might have been reasonably exercised.

We are told, however, that Jesus was soon after arrested in a mysterious manner by a party with lanterns, torches, and weapons, who professed to be officers and servants of the chief priests, but were evidently in the service of the Nazarenes. The account of Peter cutting off the ear of Malchus without being struck or punished in return, if not mythical, can only be explained as a piece of acting (John xviii. 10). The singular part played by

Judas Iscariot in this arrest is a clear indication that the whole was a dramatic proceeding designed to serve the purpose of the Nazarenes. Had Judas been a real traitor employed by the chief priests to compass his master's destruction, he would have been persuaded to poison him or strangle him while he slept, or at least to betray him into the hands of some other secret murderer. The mere act of kissing Jesus and pointing him out in the midst of his disciples when he was well known and did not attempt to conceal himself, would have afforded no help whatever to his religious opponents who might wish to arrest him, and could only have been useful to those who were getting up impressive spectacles and furnishing proofs of his Messiahship. Joseph of Arimathæa, and other secret heads of the sect, would naturally desire to test the Apostles and see if they were likely to be induced by any worldly considerations to abandon their cause. Under the pretence of being adversaries of Jesus, they probably conversed with them separately for the purpose of proving their real sentiments, and if they found one lacking in faith or inclined to apostatise, they would deem it advisable to anticipate his defection and eject him from his office as a perpetual example of punished faithlessness, which could in no way have been better effected than in the treatment of Judas. That this man was not a very sincere and devoted follower of Jesus is quite probable, but that he should suddenly become so wicked and reckless as to plot his master's ruin is highly improbable. The story that he went of his own accord to the chief priests and covenanted to reveal Jesus to them for thirty pieces of silver is absurd, for they would not have given a penny for such an idle service. But on the supposition that one of the Nazarene party, pretending to be a servant of the chief priests, came and offered the condemned disciple money to accompany him to a place where Jesus was waiting and salute him with a kiss, the alleged act of betrayal is perfectly intelligible. The simple and unfortunate man would readily comply with such an offer, not imagining that any harm would result from it till the formal act of salutation was accomplished, when he would suddenly find himself pointed at by his apostolic brethren, spurned, and cast off as a traitor.

Not only is the arrest of Jesus a very strange proceeding, but his trial, as reported by the Evangelists, is still more anomalous and utterly at variance with the judicial customs of the city. The real Caiaphas and Pilate could no more have taken part in such an outrageous travesty of justice than the real Moses and Elias could have been present on the mountain in Galilee. Had Jesus been arrested by the Temple magistracy and tried by them in concert with the procurator they would have been sure to charge him with his recent breach of the peace, and some of the merchants who were scourged would have been called on to confront him and state their grievances. But it is made to appear that the judges before whom he was brought were so silly, and at the same time so corrupt, that they quite overlooked or forgot his real offence, while they bribed false witnesses to bring against him a number of irrelevant charges which were absolutely worthless. If such a judicial farce was actually witnessed in Jerusalem, if the proceedings against Jesus were as irregular and unreasonable as they are described in the Gospel narrative, we may be quite sure that his trial was a mock trial, and he must have been brought before a fictitious Sanhedrin composed of men who, while acting as his enemies, were really confederated Nazarenes.

The presumption that the trial of Jesus was a dramatic performance for party purposes is greatly strengthened by its manifestly one-sided character, by its being throughout all accusation and no defence. There is no conflict of witnesses, no striving of pleaders for opposite verdicts as we invariably see in a genuine trial; not a single voice from among sympathising friends is raised for acquittal, but all present are represented as being actively or passively in favour of condemnation. If the proceedings were really such as they are described by the Evangelists, this singular concurrence of all engaged therein to send Jesus to an ignominious death could only have resulted from their being an organised party whose real object was to exhibit the Jewish authorities in a bad light and render them altogether odious. Viewed as a dramatic performance, it is also easy to understand the fickleness of the people—probably few in number, though supposed to be a multitude—who demonstrated with palm-branches before Jesus, and soon after wanted him crucified; their change of feeling was not real, but merely assumed for the occasion. This most strange and irregular trial is said to have taken place at night, which would naturally be the fittest time for a clandestine court to meet, whereas we know that the genuine Sanhedrin could not hold its sittings in the night nor on any day preceding a Sabbath or public feast. Modern Jewish scholars declare that the trial of Jesus as reported by the Evangelists is so completely at variance with the regulations of the Sanhedrin, that it could not possibly have taken place before that court. Dr. Benisch writes:—

"All prescribed formalities for the protection of a prisoner were not only disregarded, but some of them even grossly violated, and the accused was condemned for what was no crime at all by the Jewish law. To conclude that there was a Jewish trial, we have to assume that the Sanhedrin which condemned Jesus undertook an utterly useless and even senseless task, as a Jewish court at the time had no longer the power to carry out its sentence; that this court was presided over by Caiaphas, the high priest, consequently of the seed of Aaron, when we know from history that the presidency of the court was hereditary in the family of Hillel, certainly not descended from priests, and are acquainted with the name of every one of these functionaries until the court was closed by the Romans long after Christianity had become dominant. The succession in the family of Hillel was only once interrupted for some years after the destruction of the Temple, when the Rabbi Yochanan ben Saccai, owing to the youth of the legitimate Prince, acted as president. We must further assume that the court met again on the morrow, the first day of Passover, when it is known that the Sanhedrin were not allowed to hold a trial on Sabbaths and Festivals, or even to commence the day before, or to sit in judgment during the night. . . . We have further to believe, as we are informed in one of the Gospels, that witnesses were suborned to give false testimony, and that nevertheless those who suborned them bungled so much that the evidence could not be received by a suborning court determined to find the accused guilty. We are further to believe that these witnesses, although convicted of a falsehood in a cause involving capital punishment, were suffered to go scot-free, although the law under such circumstances distinctly prescribed that they should receive the punishment which would have been inflicted on the prisoner had he been condemned by their evidence. We are further to assume that the prisoner was ultimately found guilty on his own evidence, when the criminal code distinctly enacted that no one could be convicted on his own evidence." ("Judaism and Christianity," pp. 31, 32).

A distinguished Christian scholar, Dr. Geikie, declares that the trial which the Evangelists report was not conducted according to the well-known regulations of the Sanhedrin. He describes the constitution of the Sanhedrin, which was clearly framed in a generous spirit and for the manifest purpose of tempering justice with mercy, and goes on to say:—

"Rules so precise and so humane condemn the whole trial of Jesus before Caiaphas as an outrage. It was in fact an anticipation of the prostitution of justice which Josephus records as common in the latter days of Jerusalem. 'Fictitious tribunals and judicatures,' he tells us, 'were set up and men called together to act as judges, though they had no real authority, when it was desired to secure the death of an opponent.' As in these latter instances, so now in the case of Jesus, they kept up the form and mockery of a tribunal to the close" ("Life of Christ," p. 680).

Dr. Geikie is quite right in presuming that Jesus was brought before a mock tribunal, but he is mistaken in the belief that such a fictitious court was presided over by the genuine Caiaphas. The mock Sanhedrin which Josephus speaks of as being instituted during an insurrection at Jerusalem ("War." iv. v. 4) was not set up by the chief priests and rulers but by their revolutionary enemies, who even went so far as to kill without trial Annas, the brother-in-law of Caiaphas. A state of utter lawlessness then existed in the city for a short time, a disorderly mob got the upper hand, and much blood was shed. When Jesus came there with his disciples at the Passover season tranquillity reigned, the governing power was not upset, and the open perpetration of outrages in defiance of the constituted authorities would have been impossible. It is very evident, therefore, that the fictitious tribunal which professed to try Jesus in the night-time was simply a dramatic exhibition intended to caricature the genuine Sanhedrin before select witnesses and bring it into discredit.

Those critics who believe the trial of Jesus to have been a real trial, while they cannot accept the Evangelists' description of it as strictly accurate and trustworthy, are accustomed to reject whatever seems most unreasonable as mythical. Thus Keim considers it very unlikely that Pilate's wife would report a remarkable dream which she had experienced respecting Jesus, or that Pilate himself, being a Roman, would adopt the Jewish custom of washing hands as a symbolical protestation of innocence (Matt. xxvii. 19-24). The fact of these statements being only found in the Gospel of Matthew renders it, in his opinion, all the more probable that they are legendary interpolations. He may be quite right in his view, but it is impossible to say with confidence of these and some other statements confined to one Gospel whether they are interpolations or not. We, who regard the trial as simply a dramatic exhibition for party purposes, are not so much compelled to treat every unreasonable incident as a creation of fancy, because the unreasonable may appear in a drama as well as in a legend. Evidently the real Pilate would not have washed his hands in conformity with the Jewish custom, but one personating the procurator might have done so, and the admonitory dream might possibly have been reported by a Jewish woman acting as his wife. Whether these details originated from dramatic or poetic invention, Nazarene ideas are therein imputed to Roman minds and for a very intelligible purpose.

§ 4.—*The Resurrection.*

The Trial and Crucifixion which the Evangelists report was followed by another masked drama of supernatural character to which the Church has always attached supreme importance. When Canon W. H. Fremantle had an article in the *Fortnightly Review* a few years ago showing that miracles were thought much less of than formerly, and that belief in them had become a matter of comparative indifference, Dean Payne-Smith in a sermon on the subject declared that it was at least essential to believe in one miracle—the resurrection of Christ. But there are many thoughtful Christians who are quite unable to do so in the old orthodox sense; they can only bring themselves to believe at the utmost in a sort of spiritual resurrection. They admit that the disciples entertained a belief that their departed master was physically restored to life, but think that they were led to do so on what must now be considered insufficient evidence. This is a very reasonable opinion: it is not to be supposed that appearances, which were regarded as supernatural by the simple childlike saints of the primitive Church, would be estimated in precisely the same way if witnessed by modern Christians armed with the careful training and intelligence of a scientific age.

The Galilean brethren did not simply hold the modern Christian belief that the dead will at some time or other return to life; they thought that this great reversal of the order of nature was just then about to happen, and were under a complete resurrection craze. They were quite assured that doomsday was close upon them, that the angel of the great Judgment would shortly descend and call all the past generations of men from their graves. Their minds were in such a state of feverish excitement and expectancy in reference to this predicted event that they were ill-fitted for critical observation or any careful investigation of facts. Indeed, it was thought that the anticipated resurrection had actually begun; reports were current that several persons who were known to have died had come back to life and were again walking on earth. People went forth on a journey thinking it quite possible that they might meet on the way some dear departed relative whose loss they had mourned. And some left their homes altogether and relinquished their employments to be in readiness for the impending crash; they often looked towards heaven for signs of the general dissolution, and listened early and late for the angel's great trumpet-blast which should summon them and all other mortals to give an account of their lives.

The only evidence which the Nazarenes and others had for this strange belief which so strongly influenced them were certain forged predictions which had been written during the excitement of the Maccabean wars. Jewish mystics of that period had only got to compose prophetic visions of a sensational character and antedate them or ascribe them to holy men who had lived long before, and their inventions were accepted readily by their more credulous countrymen as revelations from Heaven. It was not considered necessary to enquire carefully into the origin and history of such writings, as was done recently in the case of the Shapira manuscript —their own representations were thought to be an amply sufficient voucher for their genuineness. And people so destitute of critical discernment who could thus believe in a coming general resurrection on the authority of spurious books, would be likely to believe in special resurrections taking place among them on the warrant of evidence that was equally weak and unreliable.

When a credulous community are hungering greatly for what they cannot possibly obtain, their unreasonable demand is pretty sure to create a fictitious supply. During the two centuries which preceded the destruction of Jerusalem, a large portion of the Jewish people were constantly prying into the future with intense eagerness and pondering over the probable destiny of their nation. To satisfy this craving there appeared from time to time the Book of Daniel, the Book of Enoch, the Assumption of Moses, the Sibylline oracles, and other apocalyptic revelations. The Christians of a later period were not so much desirous to know the future as to bring back and recover the golden past; they would gladly have seen Christ and the Apostles reappear on earth, and they hoped at least that they might behold their traces. It was for the gratification of their pious wishes that all kinds of relics were continually unearthed in a mysterious manner, and the "holy places" at Jerusalem, Bethlehem, and Nazareth were wondrously revealed. Pilgrimages and relic-worship passed away to a great extent with the Reformation, but when other illusions arose, sympathetic craft obligingly waited on credulity. John Wesley and his followers greatly wanted to witness a revival of the Apostolic miracles, and it was not long before some members of the community feigned sickness and madness in order that marvellous cures and exorcisms might be actually exhibited. During the last fifty years, in America and most other countries there has been felt an intense longing for communion with departed spirits, and ingenious persons quite equal to the occasion have produced rappings and written messages in an astonishing manner. It is well known, too, that some who have thus helped on the movement by stratagem firmly believe in spiritual manifestations, and are honest, trustworthy people, in the ordinary transactions of life. In the primitive Galilean Church it was not so much the spirits of departed friends that were looked for as their risen bodies: it was confidently expected that those who were dead and buried would soon reappear in the flesh. And if there had been nothing contrived and put forward to meet this demand it would have been truly wonderful—the ingenious would have shown a lack of sympathy with the credulous and a disinclination to humour them unknown to any other age.

A modern jury of scientific witnesses would not be satisfied that the resurrection of a buried person to new life was really accomplished unless they had two distinct proofs presented to them—a proof of death, and a proof of identity; and in all the recorded miracles of this kind there has never been furnished but one proof. You may have death without identity, or identity without death, in the miracle which you are permitted to witness, but you will not have them both. Some Eastern magicians at the present day profess to kill rabbits, pigeons, and other small animals and restore them to life, but either the animal is not really killed, or when dead it is quickly concealed and a live one is introduced in its place. It is easy enough to stupefy an animal by the administration of a drug so as to render it dead in appearance, and then to revivify it under the eyes of the spectators. If they are not satisfied as to life being extinct, the magicians will give the most complete proof of death by decapitation, but in such case the restoration process is not witnessed. The head and trunk of the dead animal, after being held up to view, are thrown into a basket or some other receptacle, and there presently emerges a live one which is supposed to be the same; yet what intelligent witness would under such circumstances be induced to swear to its identity? Nothing superior to these unsatisfactory performances in respect to completeness has ever been exhibited in the miraculous restoration of human life

We are told that Jesus during his public ministry raised up three deceased persons, the daughter of

Jairus, the son of a widow, and Lazarus of Bethany, but allowing these cases to be historical and correctly reported, there is in neither of them any proof of death. Lazarus, according to the Johannine narrative, had been four days buried, not in a close grave, but in a habitable cavern, where it might have been possible for a hermit to abide a long while in comfortable seclusion. People have been much worse buried, they have been miserably entombed under snowdrifts and in deep mines for upwards of a fortnight, and then have been dug out and completely restored. Still more wonderful are those well-authenticated cases of Hindoo ascetics buried for several weeks in a state of suspended animation and then disinterred and brought back to life. Such cases are not supernatural, but they have a better claim to be considered miracles than the five or six instances of raising the dead ascribed to St. Francis Xavier in India, or than any of the resurrection performances of the primitive Church. If a modern Lazarus, in obedience to some preacher's call, were now to come out of a tomb wrapped about with grave-clothes, it would be considered a drama and not a miracle.

The resurrection of Jesus himself differs greatly from all the other instances of raising the dead recorded by the Evangelists, because there is every reason to believe that he died in reality. It is well known that crucifixion does not produce the sure and speedy death which necessarily results from decapitation. On some occasions it appears that people have been saved after suffering in this way, as was the case with Sandokes ("Herodotus," vii. 194) the friend of Josephus ("Life," 75), and the French Convulsionaries of the last century. If the newspapers are to be believed, a woman recently recovered after enduring several hours of crucifixion in America. But in all these instances the sufferers evidently wished to recover and were glad to receive at the hands of their friends timely assistance. On the other hand, Jesus desired to die as a fulfiller of Scripture; he had made serious and deliberate arrangements for that purpose, all his hopes were centred on the termination of his earthly career, and a rescue from the jaws of death would have been to him a cruel disappointment.

Those theorists who believe that Jesus was buried in an unconscious state and was presently revived by the coolness of the tomb and enabled to walk forth and present himself again to the disciples, cling to the notion that he was actually crucified by his enemies. According to their view his resurrection was not calculated on at all, it was purely a physiological accident. The Evangelists, however, assure us that when Jesus had conversed with two mysterious persons on a mountain in Galilee respecting "his decease which he should accomplish at Jerusalem," he expressly told his disciples that "on the third day he should be raised again." The rising, as well as the crucifixion, was evidently planned by his confederated partisans, and the whole performance was carried out on their grounds. Had he been put to death by his enemies, the execution would probably have taken place on some wild barren spot near the city, certainly not close to a garden and one singularly provided with a new tomb. We are told that the chief priests and rulers knew well that he had promised to rise again after three days, and being apprehensive that the disciples would steal away the body to make it appear that he had risen, were resolved to do all in their power to prevent it. But had such been the case, would they have allowed the body to be delivered into the custody of Joseph of Arimathæa when they might have taken it to some very secure place of their own? As Jesus was considered not permanently dead, as it was expected that he would escape from the tomb in a few days, or that another person would go forth and act as the risen Jesus, his enemies under such circumstances would have regarded and treated him as a prisoner. And certainly no people in their right senses would think of sending a prisoner of war for safe custody to a castle belonging to his own partisans, even if trustworthy soldiers were posted at the gate. The story of the Jewish rulers conferring with the Roman procurator as to the best means of making a resurrection impossible and blundering to such an extent is absurd; they were evidently not in the business at all, nor in the least aware of what was being done. As Joseph had the disposal of the body, we may be quite sure that he was the master of the whole dramatic exhibition; the garden and the tomb were in his possession, and those who performed their respective parts there as angels from Heaven, and as soldiers of Cæsar, were entirely under his command.

When the angels, or white-robed men acting as such, came to the sepulchre while it was dark to take away the body, the dramatic soldiers posted there would of course be directed to go forthwith into the city and report the resurrection of Jesus. They were perhaps frightened, imagining that real angels had appeared to them, and so would readily do as they were told. But the story of their going to the chief priests and rulers to deliver their message, and being bribed by the Sanhedrin to report a falsehood is altogether absurd (Matt. xxviii. 12). "It is a difficulty," says Strauss, "acknowledged even by orthodox expositors, that the Sanhedrin in a regular assembly and after a formal consultation should have resolved to corrupt the soldiers and put a lie into their mouths. That in this manner a college of seventy men should have officially decided on suggesting and rewarding the utterance of a falsehood is too widely at variance with the decorum, the sense of propriety inseparable from such an assembly."

Moreover, the council must have known that the lie for which they are said to have given "large money" would have been utterly worthless for advancing their own ends or obstructing the cause of their opponents. If they had deemed the report of the resurrection false, they would have thought it better to examine the men publicly and expose their mendacity than pay them to contradict one lie by the utterance of another which no sensible person would believe. On the other hand, if they had been convinced of the truth of the miracle, they would have been further convinced that Jesus would soon by his personal presence among the people give any report which might be circulated of the stealing of his body a triumphant refutation. Such an extremely gross charge advanced against the Jewish rulers, making them out to be at once the vilest of scoundrels and the flattest of fools, only indicates that those from whom it proceeded were strongly prejudiced and were not very scrupulous or actuated by a high sense of honour themselves.

When the "soldiers" had gone away into the city, the "angels" had the sepulchre to themselves and could soon remove the body, which was probably taken to some other prepared spot in the garden and there deposited permanently. But two of them remained at the empty vault to inform the disciples, who were expected to arrive at daybreak, that Jesus was risen from the dead (Luke xxiv. 4; John xx. 12). One of the Nazarene confederacy was now appointed to personate Jesus before some of the leading disciples, as they had previously personated Moses and Elias on a mountain in Galilee. We are informed, at least, that a mysterious stranger presented himself to a few privileged beholders in that character. It is commonly supposed that this unknown man, who appeared to the disciples after the evacuation of the sepulchre, was believed by them to be

Jesus, on the ground of his perfect identity in form and feature with their late master. Thus Dr. Wardlaw writes:—

"They had long intimate familiar acquaintance with their master previous to his death and up to the time of his death. They had associated with him constantly for three years. They knew him in every feature of his countenance and every member of his frame, in every attitude, every gesture, every look, every tone of voice, in every particular by which it is conceivable that personal identity can be ascertained; and having thus known him there was no interval of subsequent separation to weaken their impressions or obscure their reminiscences of him. Suppose our most intimate friend to die—to die not by a lingering and wasting process of dissolution, but by a sudden death in his full strength, without tedious emaciation or aught that could induce any alteration in his ordinary appearance; suppose him to continue dead from Friday afternoon till Sunday morning, and then to appear to us, not in vision but really and corporally his *bonâ fide* self; is it possible, think you, that in so short a time we could so have forgotten him as to be even in the slightest degree at a loss to recognise him and to be sure of his identity?" (On "Miracles," ch. iv., sec. 4).

Certainly not; we would undertake to say that there is not a Sadducee in the whole country who would fail to recognise his risen friend instantly under such circumstances. And it must be borne in mind that the disciples had not so much antecedent unbelief in people coming from their graves as there now exists among modern Christians; a resurrection was not deemed in those days an impossible or very extraordinary occurrence. When Lazarus, after being buried or concealed four days in a cave, came forth wrapped about in burial-clothes as one restored to life, the people who had been invited to witness his rising, as well as those who came to see him afterwards, appear to have had no doubt whatever as to his being the genuine Lazarus of Bethany. They recognised him readily enough, and the only misgiving likely to arise in their minds was as to the reality of his death. In the case of Jesus the opposite side of an imperfect miracle was exhibited; the disciples had been present to witness his death, but his rising was secret, and when at length a living person appeared to them, professing to be their late master, they had much difficulty to believe in his identity.

When the supposed Jesus presented himself to Mary Magdalene, so far from being recognised instantly "in every feature of his countenance," we are told that she took him to be the gardener and addressed him as such (John xx. 15). He afterwards fell in with two disciples who were going to Emmaus, and, as they believed their new companion to be a stranger, he exhibited considerable skill in forcing from them a recognition. He did not present at once all his "infallible proofs" so as to run the risk of failure, but began by sounding them and preparing their minds for belief. "Ought not Christ to have suffered these things?" said he, and then "expounded unto them in all the scriptures the things concerning himself" (Luke xxiv. 26, 27). He was evidently a man of more craft and learning than the humble carpenter of Nazareth who had been artfully led on to fulfil Scripture and sacrifice his life. The simple disciples were at length induced to believe that their companion was no other than Jesus by his peculiar manner of breaking and blessing bread, which served as a sort of masonic sign to accredit him when they had entirely failed to recognise him by any natural attitude or feature.

In the evening of that day, when other disciples

were assembled with closed doors conversing on their master's reappearance, we are told he suddenly "stood in the midst of them and saith, Peace be unto you. But they were terrified and affrighted and supposed that they had seen a spirit" (Luke xxiv. 36, 37). They were probably assembled on this occasion at the same convenient house of the Nazarene confederacy where they had eaten the Passover and where they afterwards met on the Day of Pentecost. The personator of Jesus might have been in another room so as to overhear their conversation and learn the current of their thoughts, and then at a favourable moment he would only have to rush in among them by a sudden *coup de théâtre* and exhibit his pierced hands and feet to make them well assured of his identity. But the very fact of his exhibiting these artificial features and making them prominent, and relying on them as the best evidence that he had to offer, is a clear indication that he did not bear with him the true distinguishing marks of nature. In a modern court of justice the presentation of wounds or scars to establish a person's identity as a claimant is always regarded with the greatest suspicion. Moreover, if Jesus had actually risen from the dead, his wounds which were the cause of his death ought to have been healed, and he should have come forth from the sepulchre and presented himself perfectly sound and whole. A man could no more live with a deep spear-wound in his pericardium than he could with his throat cut or his head severed from his body; in order that life should return, the damage inflicted on him must be thoroughly repaired. Evidently the wounds which served to convince the credulous disciples were merely skin-wounds or *stigmata*, such as those which several saints contrived to imprint on themselves in mediæval times. A person pierced in that superficial manner would not be disabled, and might even move about with very little difficulty or inconvenience.

Jesus had been instructed by the confederacy not only to predict his rising from the dead, but to appoint a place in Galilee where he would meet the disciples (Matt. xxvi. 32; Mark xiv. 28). Accordingly, the personator went there at the proper time to fulfil this prediction. The mountain where he appeared was probably that on which the pretended Moses and Elias had presented themselves a short time before. It does not seem that he came in actual contact with the disciples on this occasion, but the evidence of identity relied on was his appearing exactly in the place where Jesus had promised to appear. He probably spoke to them at a little distance off, habited in a white garment suitable for one supposed to have risen from the dead. But simple and credulous as the disciples were with regard to illusory appearances, and with every preparation being made to induce them to believe that their late master now stood before them, we are told that "some doubted" (Matt. xxviii. 17).

The slowness of the disciples to believe in the person who appeared before them as the risen Jesus, forms a difficulty which is freely admitted by most orthodox commentators. Some modern writers, who reject the supernatural view, attempt to account for it in this way: they believe that Jesus was buried in a state of swoon, and was presently revived with kind nursing and enabled to escape from the tomb with a fresh supply of clothes. Through being disguised in this way that he might not be observed and recaptured by his enemies, the disciples whom he met were unable to recognise him. This explanation is not a very reasonable one. For supposing Jesus to have been crucified and buried in a state of coma, he must have been in such a precarious condition from his wounds that the best nursing he could have

would not have enabled him to walk for a long distance
The disciples would have expected their master to appear in fresh raiment, and the real Jesus, however clad, might have readily obtained a recognition from them if he had wanted to be recognised. Moreover, had he got away from the guarded tomb in a disguised dress as a prisoner now and then escapes from a dungeon, his enemies would have gone in pursuit of him, and some mention of the efforts they made to effect his recapture would have been sure to appear in the narrative.

Ernest Renan and other critics of his school endeavour to account for the failure of the apparitions of the risen Jesus to produce strong conviction on the theory that they were subjective visions created by the disciples' imagination. Albert Reville, writing on the subject recently, says : " Jesus is not recognised, or they doubt whether it is really he ; little by little the conviction of the witnesses takes form and strengthens. Even when he is finally recognised, they are still afraid that it is only an apparition devoid of the tangible reality. At last conviction carries the day" (*The New World*, Sept., 1894). There is really no substantial ground for this opinion. Jesus and his disciples were not mystics or men of strong creative fancy. They looked confidently for the approaching resurrection of the dead, and the apparitions which so strongly influenced them were evidently objective. The figures which they saw were of precisely the same realistic character as that of the Virgin Mary, who appeared some years ago to peasant children on the mountain of La Salette. Such apparitions only occur in obscure places and under the eyes of a few favoured spectators who are extremely simple and credulous. The Apostle Paul might be considered a mystic; he undoubtedly had visions occasionally of his own making (Acts xxii. 17 ; 2 Cor. xii. 1-4), but we have reason to believe that it was a dramatic apparition of the risen Jesus that effected his conversion.

It is evident that two quite different orders of people were engaged in constructing the Nazarene Church—men of craft, and men of credulity—and it is only from a few of the latter that our very meagre information on the subject is derived. They have reported certain appearances which seemed to them supernatural, but some of the attendant circumstances are of such a character as to excite suspicion, and there cannot be a doubt that shrewder minds played on their simplicity. And these more intelligent members of the community, who could have given a much fuller and better account of the origin of the Christian faith than any that we now possess, chose for special reasons of their own to keep in the background and maintain a discreet silence. If the secrets that were known to the rich Arimathæan and his plotting associates had only come out at Jerusalem, it is highly probable that both he and they would have been arrested and tried by the order of the procurator, and on his own grounds there might soon have been exhibited a second and more public crucifixion to serve as an atonement for the first.

It is curious to observe in the history of religious movements how earnest-minded people, when carried away by a mistaken belief, have often resorted to stratagem for the purpose of forcing their illusions on others. The unknown author of the Book of Daniel was doubtless fully convinced in his own mind that there would soon come a general resurrection and judgment, to be followed by the establishment of a Kingdom of Heaven. But not content with simply telling people that such were his views and anticipations, he resolved to convince them more effectively by writing prophetic visions, which should have the appearance of being composed long before his time. This artifice was a great success;

it imposed on many of his educated countrymen, and the belief which he and a few other visionaries entertained thus gradually became diffused among the Pharisee and Essene portions of the community. The mysterious Book of Daniel was well studied by Jewish mystics during the Roman domination; the rich Arimathæan must have read and pondered over it a good deal, and have been thoroughly convinced of its genuineness. And he resembled the author in having a disposition to strengthen his belief and render it more acceptable to other people by stratagem. He might have written prophetic visions of a similar kind for this purpose and ascribed them to Moses, Elias, or some other ancient Israelite. And his forged book would doubtless have gradually got into circulation and obtained credit, as others had done, although not to any great extent in his lifetime. Being a man of great dramatic genius, he took a bolder course; he resolved to provide object-lessons which should influence directly the credulous illiterate class who were not able to read books. Thousands of peasants and others had heard that a resurrection of the dead was foretold without being greatly affected by such a dim prospective miracle; how much more strongly would they be impressed and moved if risen men could only be brought before their eyes! It was to this argumentative method of working upon their minds that the Arimathæan directed his inventiveness; he turned his garden into a theatre, waged a dramatic war against the Sanhedrin, caused angels and departed saints to appear as occasion required, and in a very brief time outdid all the faith-forming illusionment that had ever been accomplished by the Grecian mysteries.

We are told that the patriarch Jacob succeeded in depriving Esau of his birthright by illusory appearances, and in much the same way did this crafty Joseph long afterwards seek to upset the authority of the legitimate rulers of Israel. It cannot be denied that he was terribly unjust towards the Sanhedrin; but he does not seem to have been an ambitious, self-seeking adventurer; he was willing to spend his wealth freely, and completely efface himself for the advancement of what he considered a good cause. He was probably under the impression that the coming of the promised Kingdom of Heaven would be delayed till there was seen a sufficient preparation for it in the establishment of a great believing community. Hence it was thought desirable to use all possible means of convincing people and getting them to stand in readiness for the Judgment as good world-renouncing saints. He deceived people as he thought for their welfare just as many others did at that period, and it is quite possible that he helped to save many poor visionaries from their own worse illusions. When simple, unsuspecting persons are commercially cheated we may reasonably pity them, and strongly denounce the fraud that has been practised upon them, for we know that they have been taken advantage of against their own will. It is very different, however, when they are imposed upon by religious and political teachers, as they have been more or less in every age, for then they get simply what is agreeable to them, what is most satisfactory to their minds. And if any honest friend endeavours to undeceive them and bring them to apprehend the plain naked truth, his well-intended efforts only irritate them and fill them with passionate resentment. They say in effect to all who are disposed to instruct them, "We want none of your sober verities, but such things as afford us pleasurable excitement. Let us have many astonishing miracles; continually hold before us bright millennial promises; give us visions and voices from Heaven!"

CHAPTER III.

THE CLOAK OF MARTYRDOM.

§ 1.—*The Significant Silence.*

IN the foregoing chapters we have explained the trial, crucifixion, and resurrection of Jesus as a dramatic scheme devised and carried out entirely by his own partisans. They believed that what Isaiah had written of the sorrows of Israel in a condition of exile pointed prophetically to a suffering Messiah, and therefore thought that Jesus, as the anointed one, must necessarily experience similar ill-treatment. A greater mistake in respect to a writer's meaning could hardly have been made, and the notion that an individual must suffer, precisely as a captive nation had suffered, was to the last degree unreasonable. In ancient times nations were continually at strife, and being restrained by no international law, they treated one another with the greatest cruelty and injustice. The Israelites conquered and oppressed every neighbouring people weaker than themselves, and they were at length subdued in turn and made to suffer much by the stronger Chaldeans. Then, instead of reflecting that they were only being served as they had often enough served others, they began to whine over their troubles as though there were no other people in the world ever treated so badly as they were. And the best explanation that they could give of the Chaldean bondage, in their self-righteous conceit, was that God had somehow delivered them up to be punished in this way for other people's iniquities.

For an individual Jew to suffer such treatment from his countrymen as the captive nation had suffered at the hands of the Gentiles, he would have to be of the lawless predatory class. We can imagine a Jewish robber, having a considerable amount of success, committing many aggressions on his neighbours, and bringing home from time to time abundance of spoil. But at length a powerful band of robbers fall upon him, and not only seize his goods, but carry him right off beyond the borders with his wife and children, and sell them all into slavery. Such a man might greatly deplore his fate, and might justly say that his case of suffering was exactly parallel to that which the nation had endured in Chaldea. Jesus, however, was a poor, honest citizen under the protection of the Law, and in no danger whatever of experiencing such treatment. He lived, too, in peaceable times when the country was free from tumults, and law-abiding people had nothing to apprehend from partisan violence. But those who thought that he was portrayed in the figurative language of Isaiah as the Messiah, believed that it was absolutely necessary for the fulfilment of Scripture that he should at least suffer unjustly in appearance. Hence the arrest and mock trial, and all the dramatic exhibition designed to make him seem the victim of his religious opponents, especially to make it believed that he was plotted against and persecuted by the Jewish authorities. His terrible wrongs and afflictions were got up to serve a purpose, were skilfully manufactured to tally with what had been written, and thus furnish an incontestable proof of his Messiahship. It will be believed by the Christian multitude for centuries to come that Pilate and the Jewish rulers were responsible for his crucifixion, but they had clearly nothing whatever to do with it, and could not have been aware that a cruel exhibition, manifestly designed to cast discredit on themselves, had occurred near the city. We propose now to set forth in order the whole of the reasons which compel us to consider them innocent of the charge advanced against them by the primitive Church.

Modern Christians have come to entertain the belief that the Calvary transaction was an atrocious case of regicide, just as notorious and indisputable at the time of its occurrence as the assassination of Cæsar. But Jesus held no regal position in the world to render his dying by violence a sensational tragedy to provoke wide and general comment. He was simply a Galilean peasant with a small following, an obscure claimant of spiritual sovereignty, and at the time of his death only a very small portion of his countrymen could have had any knowledge of his existence. Beyond his own circle so little interest was felt in the crucifixion which he is said to have suffered, or so little was known of it by intelligent people likely to be moved by acts of monstrous injustice that, according to general opinion, not a word was written about it till some thirty or forty years after its occurrence. Yet, with the immense growth of the Christian Church, imagination has so magnified this obscure event that we now continually hear it spoken of as being "the greatest crime of history."

Why do we believe that in the seventeenth century Charles I. was put to death by a dominant portion of the people of England, and that in the following century Louis XVI. was dealt with in the same way by a dominant portion of the people of France? Chiefly for these reasons: We know, in the first place, that a vast number of people, that is, the whole republican party of each country, expected to profit much by their king's death; they considered him their most dangerous enemy, and the greatest obstacle to the carrying out of their revolutionary designs. Then we have streaming down upon us a wide flood of contemporary evidence, the testimony in each case not only of both parties therein directly concerned—the friends and foes of the suffering monarch—but of numerous other persons who looked on calmly, and commented on the tragic proceedings from an independent position. The tribunals that tried the two kings were stigmatised as murderers by millions of people opposed to their views; they admitted themselves that they were responsible for what was being done, and put on record their reasons for taking the course which they did, so as to justify themselves as far as possible in the eyes of posterity.

We have no corresponding volume of evidence to convince us that Jesus was cruelly persecuted and condemned to death by the Jewish Sanhedrin. He held no public position, and the Jews could have no rational motive for killing him with the view to effect a change in their government. He was not a dangerous or obnoxious character to render his removal desirable; no party was in the least likely to benefit by his death; and, if the Evangelists speak truly of the amount of healing which he did, the whole community must have been interested in prolonging his life. The only direct testimony that we have of his falling a victim to the malice of the Sanhedrin is furnished by those few sectarian chroniclers who evidently regarded the Jewish rulers with intense hostility. Not a single word in support of their accusation has come down to us from other Jewish sects, neither have we the smallest amount of corroborative testimony from Roman, Greek, Syrian, or Samaritan. If the Sanhedrin had really condemned Jesus to death, they must have given some reason for doing so, they would have felt bound to commit to writing the best possible justification of their conduct, and a forged declaration to that effect (the work of some Christian) was actually produced in the primitive Church, but there is no trace of a genuine document having ever existed. So far as we can learn, neither they nor any who upheld their authority once acknowledged that they were responsible for the Crucifixion which took place on the grounds of the rich Arimathæan, and their alleged guilt is strongly denied at the present day by all the most able and respected leaders of the Jewish community.

In the modern popular conception, what the Evangelists or their informants beheld at Calvary was an event of surpassing magnitude; all nature was convulsed by it: the sun was darkened, the earth quaked, the rocks rent, the graves were opened, and there was a partial rising of the dead (Matt. xxviii. 51, 52; Luke xxiii. 24, 25). These stupendous wonders, as *The Christian World* has recently admitted, were clearly produced by imagination alone; they form an emblazonment of myths which gathered about the original report, and there was a tendency to add to them continually. It has been repeatedly pointed out that had such miracles occurred in reality, they would have filled the whole world with astonishment and formed a universal topic for all the historians, philosophers, and poets of that age. During the second century it was felt by Christian writers that great trouble and consternation must necessarily have been produced by these prodigies, and therefore mythical results which seemed likely to have happened were recorded. The Gospel of Peter in its account of the darkness which overspread the land says: "And many went about with lamps supposing that it was night, and fell down. . . . Then the Jews and the elders and the priests, seeing what evil they had done to themselves, began to lament and to say, Woe for our sins, for the judgment and the end of Jerusalem hath drawn nigh." In a later legendary document purporting to be an account of the Crucifixion sent by Pilate to the Emperor Tiberius, the procurator is made to say that even Cæsar himself must be aware "that in all the world they lighted lamps from the sixth hour until evening" ("Anaphora Pilati," B. c. 7).

But without the added prodigies, and regarded simply as a judicial crime perpetrated by the Roman and Jewish authorities, the Crucifixion would have been an astounding occurrence calculated to produce at once an immense sensation in the world. There is nothing that so powerfully affects the popular mind and gets so speedily blazed abroad in all directions as a deed of remorseless cruelty. For an atrocity of exceptional wickedness to be witnessed in open day without its becoming everywhere notorious in a very short time would be morally impossible. It is the known absence of such a result in the case of the Massacre of the Innocents that has caused so many investigators to reject that story as legendary. When the crucifixion of Jesus is said to have been a great public spectacle at Jerusalem, many Jews were assembled from all quarters to keep the Passover, and it might naturally be supposed that they would soon carry the news of it into far distant lands. In such case it could not fail to impress thoughtful minds and provoke much serious comment throughout the widely-dispersed Jewish community. How is it then that there is not the slightest allusion to it anywhere in their contemporary literature? Why was there no mention of it made by such well-informed writers as Philo, Justus of Tiberias, and Josephus? During the third century inquiring Christians began to consider it strange that the latter had said nothing about it in his History, and one at length undertook to supply the supposed defect by interpolating the passage ("Ant." xviii. iii. 3) which has ever since formed a sort of spurious Gospel in miniature.

According to the genuine text of Josephus, into which this Christian testimony has been craftily vamped, the Romans in Pilate's time were accustomed to punish people with great severity, but only when they were found guilty of flagrant offences. Decius Mundus, for instance, seduced a Roman lady in the temple of Isis by personating the god Anubis with the connivance of the priests, whom he had bribed for that purpose, and on the scandal being discovered the Emperor was so provoked that he had the temple demolished, the priests crucified, and Mundus sent into exile. About the same time another credulous Roman lady named Fulvia, who had been converted to Judaism, was shamefully imposed upon by dishonest Jews, who obtained rich presents from her under the pretence of devoting them to the service of the Temple at Jerusalem, and on their fraud being found out the whole community were banished from Rome. While impostors were thus rigorously dealt with by his imperial master, Pilate himself had occasion to act with some severity against a scheming leader of armed men who was creating a disturbance in Samaria. This adventurer induced his credulous followers to believe that he would reveal to them the sacred vessels deposited by Moses on Mount Gerizzim; and, like other finders of holy relics, he had doubtless hidden away himself what he intended to discover. Pilate, hearing of his plan for cajoling ignorant people, and apprehending evil results, hastened to Gerizzim with soldiers and at once seized on all the roads which led up to the mountain so as to render it inaccessible to the armed multitude. A struggle, therefore, ensued between the opposing parties; the misguided band of treasure-seekers were soon routed, and some who had been most active as leaders were afterwards captured and slain. The Samaritan council of elders, thinking that Pilate had acted rashly and with too great severity on this occasion, made a complaint against him to Vitellius, the President of Syria. Vitellius thereupon ordered him to proceed to Rome and answer to the Samaritan charge in the presence of the Emperor, but Tiberius died before he could arrive there (" Ant." xviii. iii. 4, 5 ; iv. i.).

Pilate may have died directly after his imperial master for anything we know, as we now completely lose sight of him. We are not told whether he succeeded in vindicating his action at Gerizzim, but, supposing that he survived Tiberius a few years—he very probably did—for all that could be reasonably said against him was, that in the opinion of the elders his dispersion of the armed multitude by force involving a sacrifice of life was unnecessary. The Roman senate would be likely to entertain a different view of the matter; had Pilate suffered the scheming revelator to ascend the mountain and unearth the sacred vessels before his astonished followers, they would have believed him to be a second Moses, and so many lawless men would have flocked to his standard that in all probability there would have followed in a little while a much greater effusion of blood. A Roman governor had a difficult part to play in such circumstances; if he failed to deal promptly with an incipient rising and suffered it to get to a head, he was charged with incapacity ; while if he took resolute measures to nip it in the bud, there was pretty sure to be a petition got up for his removal on the score of cruelty. It is evident that Pilate had to be very circumspect and mind what he was about, for both in Samaria and in Judæa there were plenty of discontented people desirous of change ready to proceed against him as accusers if any occasion was afforded them for representing that he had acted unjustly or had exceeded his legitimate authority.

If the narrative of Josephus is to be relied on, Pilate was a stern Roman soldier, a man of iron will, more likely to err on the side of severity than on that of clemency. The Evangelists, however, have made him appear a weak, vacillating character, inclined to humour the people and easily moved to act against his own interests by a little persuasion. Assuming the story which they tell of the trial and crucifixion of Jesus to be strictly correct, it is not at all likely that Pilate would have reported the disgraceful proceeding to the Emperor. He must have been ashamed to announce that he had been so feeble and irresolute as to yield to the popular clamour against his own conscience, and allow an innocent man to be treated in such a way as to bring the administration of justice into utter contempt. The report of such a flagrant magisterial scandal would have been made by his enemies; they would have spread the news of it eagerly enough in every direction, and more than one messenger would have carried it speedily to Rome. It would have been told there that the Governor of Judæa, from some unaccountable caprice, had set free a captured brigand to perpetrate further mischief, and had crucified in his stead an estimable teacher, offering at the same time an insult to the whole nation by placing over the head of the innocent victim as a superscription, "The King of the Jews." When such an outrageous transaction had come to the knowledge of the imperial authorities—and it could not have been long kept from them—they would have believed that Pilate had gone mad, and would have sent to the President of Syria a warrant to deprive him of his office immediately.

What became of this famous procurator after Vitellius ordered him to proceed to Rome nothing is known; he was not famous then, and no particular attention was directed to him. But during the third and fourth centuries much curiosity was excited about him in the now great and powerful Christian community, and to satisfy this feeling there was no authentic information. Consequently imagination was set to work in every direction to supply the need, and he became the subject of an immense number of Christian legends. The Chronicle of Melalas alleges that he was beheaded in the reign of Nero. The "Mors Pilati" says that he committed suicide, that his body was thrown into the Tiber, but as disastrous storms and floods were thereby caused, it was ultimately fished up and carried away beyond the bounds of Italy. According to one story, perhaps suggested by the fate of Archelaus, he was banished to Vienne on the Rhone, and a pyramidal monument, said to be his tomb, is still exhibited there. Another legend affirms that he sought a refuge from continual wretchedness on Mount Pilatus, near Lake Lucerne, and at length drowned himself there to end his remorse.

The whole of the extensive literature which sprung up in the primitive Church in reference to Pilate, is unquestionably mythical; it reveals the sentiments which were entertained by Christians at that period, and nothing more. Justin Martyr, Tertullian, Eusebius, and others affirm that he sent an official report of the Crucifixion to the Emperor Tiberius, but the Latin letters purporting to be such which have come down to us are universally admitted to be forgeries. Some scholars now contend that though these letters are clearly spurious, those seen by Tertullian and other eminent fathers of the Church were in all probability genuine. We have no reason for presuming such to be the case; if an authentic report from Pilate's hand had existed in the third century, it is not likely that imagination would have produced a legendary one. It is still less likely that the latter would have obtained so much readier acceptance, that the former would at length be completely lost sight of and obliterated from human remembrance. Had Pilate actually sent a report of the Crucifixion to Tiberius he must have given some justification for putting Jesus to death; he must have made it appear that the part which he had taken' in the trial and condemnation of the Jewish teacher was reasonable under the circumstances. And such a document would have been of very great importance to the Pagan community at Rome, and so serviceable in their controversy with Christian invaders that they would on no account have permitted it to perish. They would have continually set against the story which the Christians told, the authoritative testimony of Governor Pilate, and contended that the latter in the eyes of all sensible Romans was far more entitled to belief. The fact that no such appeal was made to a report of the procurator by Pagan disputants, from the reign of Nero to that of Constantine, is a clear proof that nothing of the kind had been known to exist. And what Tacitus, writing of the conflagration of Rome, says about punishment being meted out to the founder of the accused sect by Pilate, must have been derived from a Christian source. Whiston thinks that Tacitus probably got his information from Josephus. This is by no means a reasonable conjecture; but supposing the testimony, to which we have already referred, had been in the "Antiquities" at that early date, it would still be the interpolation of some Christian.

If Pilate's report of the Crucifixion would have furnished the Pagans with a good controversial weapon, that which the Sanhedrin might be expected to make for their justification would have been no less serviceable to the Jews. When Paul and other propagandists were going from city to city telling their story of the great wrong which had been perpetrated at Jerusalem, they would have been met by the cry, "*Audi alteram partem*," confronted by the different statement that had come from the Jewish authorities. A report of such immense value to the community for controversial purposes would not have been neglected or lost. It is evident, therefore, that the Sanhedrin never made a report, for the simple reason that they knew nothing whatever about the judicial murder of which they were accused. The Jews and the Romans in the first century were equally ignorant on the subject; it was only from the lips of Christians that the story of the crime was gradually promulgated throughout the world. We can only infer from this that the Crucifixion was not, as now commonly supposed, a great public spectacle, but in reality an obscure passion-drama which the followers of Jesus were alone permitted to witness. It undoubtedly took place on the private grounds of the Arimathæan, where it would have been possible to escape interruption and prevent the intrusion of strangers' eyes. For the success of such a masked drama, designed to advance the interests of a sect and discredit its opponents, seclusion would have been absolutely necessary. Had Pilate only known that the Jewish rulers and himself were being personated for the purpose of creating a prejudice in the minds of a number of credulous spectators, he would have hastened to the spot at once and broken up the show; he would have scattered the Galileans at Calvary and driven them back to the city in confusion, just as he afterwards dispersed the Samaritans at Gerizzim and frustrated in that quarter a likely scheme for influencing with illusory appearances the superstitious multitude. We shall have something more to say in reference to Pilate's alleged participation in the condemnation of Jesus to a cruel death when we come to consider the question of motives.

§ 2.—*Character of the Accused.*

In ruder times, when justice was much less satisfactorily administered, the characters of people who stood opposed to each other in a criminal charge were not properly taken into account, and the accuser was frequently permitted to have a very decided advantage over the accused. Indeed, where strong prejudice existed, it sometimes happened that men of good reputation, and even exalted position, were condemned to death on the testimony of low fellows who had always been accustomed to speak with an utter disregard for veracity. During the Middle Ages, Jewish rabbis of well-known probity had to forfeit their lives occasionally through charges trumped up against them by unprincipled wretches who wanted an excuse for plunder, or by one or two worthless renegades. And when prosecutions for witchcraft were common, several honest and well-conducted citizens were tried, condemned, and remorselessly sent to execution for being in league with the Devil on the absurd allegations of a number of silly, fanciful children. In modern judicial investigations there is more discrimination shown, and the probability of guilt is carefully weighed against the probability of misconception and untruthfulness. No person of good repute would now be convicted of a grave offence on the bare word of one who was thought to be morally his inferior. If there came to this country from China or Japan four very ardent but ill-instructed members of a new sect, who made an astonishing charge of murder against seventy national senators—men greatly superior to themselves in education and position—their story would certainly not be believed excepting by the very ignorant and credulous. Sensible people would say at once that these propagandists were far more likely to be prejudiced, mistaken, and unveracious than that seventy grave senators, accustomed to administer the laws of their country, and commanding wide and general respect, should conspire like a band of brigands to shed innocent blood.

It is only long-standing and inveterate prejudice which now causes people to believe that the Evangelists were infinitely superior in moral character to the Jewish Sanhedrin. We have no independent testimony to that effect, not a word has come down to us from Philo, Pliny, Tacitus, Seneca, and other contemporary writers to certify that one party were monsters of wickedness and the other immaculate saints. The opposing characters, as depicted by Christian tradition in their contrasted blackness and brightness, are purely legendary; imagination has formed them without the help of an atom of historical evidence. A little inquiry and reflection ought to convince everyone who is tolerably free from prejudice that the accused were not, after all, by any means so desperately vile as they have been made to appear, and that the accusers were not men of such surpassing excellence and unfaltering devotion to truthfulness that an entire reliance can be placed on their testimony.

We know that for a long time the Jews had a bad character for violence in the neighbouring Gentile world. Both Greeks and Romans regarded them as a race of fierce, sanguinary fanatics, with whom it was scarcely possible to maintain amicable relations. This, however, arose chiefly from their intense iconophobia, and their intolerance of all such forms of worship as they considered idolatry. They thought that unless they did their utmost to extirpate idolatrous practices from the land, as was done by Joshua, Elijah, Judas Maccabæus, and others, they would fail in their religious duty, and Jehovah would presently destroy them. Those who slew the worshippers of images were, in their estimation, keeping with commendable zeal the Second Commandment, and not making a breach of the Sixth. And if the immediate followers of Jesus had ventured to prostrate themselves before images and relics, as Christians got accustomed to do a few centuries afterwards, there is no doubt that they would have made themselves obnoxious to the authorities, and would have suffered as much from Puritan violence as any other idolaters. But neither Jesus, nor his disciples, nor any of his countrymen dreamt of doing such a thing, all the Jewish sects were perfectly agreed in their uncompromising hostility to idolatrous customs. A more or less strict conformity to all the regulations of the Law was required; in other respects their belief was elastic, and they did not insist on orthodox agreement. There sat, side by side, in the Sanhedrin men who differed much more widely in their religious opinions than those who now meet in the Convocation of the Church of England.

It is believed by all Christendom that the Sanhedrin was a Divine institution, that the seventy elders were the legitimate rulers of the Jewish Church, deriving their authority direct from Moses. It is known that these venerable men were the pick of the nation, that they obtained their high office solely by the recommendation of learning and worth, and that they contributed more than any other authoritative body then existing to the religious and moral education of mankind. They had the selection and keeping of a sacred literature, which, however defective it may seem to the more advanced intelligence of this age, has always been as much prized by Christians as by Jews, and is diffused at the present day in all languages throughout the whole world. On the other hand, the

Evangelists and their brethren were comparatively ignorant men, who misinterpreted the Scriptures which were put into their hands, and gave certain portions an entirely wrong meaning, and they could not be expected to judge correctly the character and aims of their learned custodians. Certainly the elders of Israel were both intellectually and morally superior to the great mass of the population, and when closely associated as a college they could not well fail to be an improving body, yet, if the Evangelists speak truly, they must have continually deteriorated in the discharge of their important duties so as to become at length the wickedest men in the world.

We know as a matter of fact that, from the time of Ezra to the time of Jesus, the Sanhedrin, with all its shortcomings, faithfully represented the progress of the nation. At no former period was it animated by a more liberal spirit than that which was imparted to it by the celebrated Hillel and his descendants. It was not infallible any more than other ecclesiastical councils have been; it placed among the sacred writings the Book of Daniel as a genuine production, when it had no better claim to be considered such than the Book of Enoch. Little wisdom was shown by the Sanhedrin in continuing to teach the prohibition of usury, and the making of images for ornamental purposes, as though they were matters of eternal obligation. And it seems to have made no serious effort to correct certain very mischievous superstitions, such as the belief in evil spirits, and the persistent attempts to read the future by sooth-saying and divination. It must be observed, however, that the Evangelists, and the early Christians generally, did not quarrel with the Sanhedrin on account of these errors and failings, for they accepted them all and went themselves still further in delusion. After poring over the prophetic visions ascribed to Daniel and Enoch, they were led to believe that the end of the world was close at hand, and that, in view of this impending catastrophe, it was prudent to abandon everything, and only study how to escape from the wreck with their lives. And if the Sanhedrin and other educated Jews had been moved by this monstrous scare to resign their occupations, sell everything they had, give the proceeds to the Communistic Church, and turn religious mendicants, no fault would have been found with their moral character. It was because they held fast to their property and went about their business as usual like sensible men, having the utmost confidence in the world's stability, that they gave so much offence, and were represented as being unbelieving, hard-hearted, covetous, hypocritical, cruel, and everything that was vile.

The distinguished French scholar, Ernest Renan, while endeavouring in his "Vie de Jesus" to reconcile the origin of Christianity with natural laws, seems to have entertained no doubt whatever respecting the fiendish malignity of the Sanhedrin. But he has tried to make it somewhat less unreasonable by charging it especially on a single member of that body. He supposes that among the assembled rulers there was one very bad man who had great influence, and that chiefly through him the others were brought to acquiesce in the shedding of innocent blood. The person whom he selects to play this ungracious part of arch-devil and persecutor is Annas, the father-in-law of Caiaphas the high-priest, and here is what he says of that ruler's character:—

"Like all the aristocracy of the temple he was a Sadducee—a sect, says Josephus, particularly severe in its judgments. All his sons also were violent persecutors. One of them named after his father, Annas, caused James, the brother of the Lord, to be stoned under circumstances not unlike those which surrounded the death of Jesus. The spirit of the family was haughty, bold, and cruel; it had that particular kind of proud and sullen wickedness which characterises Jewish politicians. Therefore, upon this Annas and his family must rest the responsibility of all the acts which followed. It was Annas (or the party he represented) who killed Jesus. Annas was the principal actor in the terrible drama, and far more than Caiaphas, far more than Pilate, ought to bear the weight of the maledictions of mankind" (Trubner's English Edition, p. 254).

This passage is wholly unworthy of a fair-minded and charitable writer like M. Renan. As an upholder of pious frauds, an inventor of persecutions, and a slanderer of men in authority, he here bears a greater resemblance to a monk of the second century than to a philosopher of the nineteenth. The only evidence, apart from the Gospels, that he is able to discover respecting Annas is in the writings of Josephus, and what that historian says of the Jewish ruler, so far from affording any ground for a belief in his extreme wickedness, is altogether favourable. "This elder Annas was a prosperous man, for he had five sons who successively filled the high-priest's office, and he had himself formerly held that dignity a long while ("Ant." xx. ix. 1). "The people having risen against the conspirators at the instance of Annas, the senior of the high priests, a man of consummate ability, who might have saved the city but for those who plotted against him" ("War" iv. iii. 7). But as M. Renan's object is to blacken his reputation, he finds it convenient to pass by this testimony, and endeavours to make it appear that he must have been a cruel persecutor, because he belonged to the Sadducee party who, Josephus says, "were severe in their judgments." The fact is that the Sadducees were in a political sense the Tories of the Jewish nation, and were not so much inclined as the Pharisees to court popularity. We are not told that they were corrupt, or partial, or inclined to punish the innocent, but only that they were more severe than their rivals in chastising the guilty. Besides, it does not follow that Annas was severe— much less unjust—because he belonged to a party that had a character for judicial severity, and neither can he be proved tyrannical by any evidence showing that tyranny prevailed in his family. But is there such evidence? "All his sons also were violent persecutors." What history records it? How does M. Renan make this out but by his own busy fable-building imagination? "One of them named like his father, Annas, caused James, the brother of the Lord, to be stoned." This is only a modern conjecture based on an ancient forgery. The words in Josephus, "James, the brother of Jesus, who was called Christ" ("Ant." xx. ix. 1), are well known by scholars to be a Christian interpolation of the fourth century, and are of no more value as evidence than the earlier and less successful interpolation quoted by Origen, which represents that the destruction of the city was acknowledged by the Jews to be a retribution which fell on them for the murder of this James.

All that we are told in the genuine text of Josephus is, that when the procurator Festus was dead, and had not been succeeded by Albinus, certain law-breakers were condemned to stoning by Annas, the high-priest, at the head of the assembled Sanhedrin. Some persons thought that Annas was too forward in this proceeding, that he had no constitutional right to take the course which he did in the absence of the Roman governor, and they complained to king Herod Agrippa on the subject. Who the law-breakers condemned on this occasion were, we cannot say with certainty, as Dr. Lardner maintains in his "Jewish Testimonies," p. 180.

But there is very little doubt that they were robbers, as that class of criminals had then become a terrible pest in Jerusalem. We are told, indeed, in this chapter of the Antiquities, that the high-priest Annas suffered terribly from their lawlessness, as they carried off his servants to obtain, by way of exchange, the release of their own captured comrades, and some of them were emboldened in their freebooting enterprises, and escaped punishment, through being related to the family of Herod Agrippa ("Ant." xx. ix. 3, 4). Not a shadow of evidence does the narrative furnish to warrant the supposition that his attempt to enforce the laws of the country at a time of emergency, without sufficient authority, was aggravated by cruelty and injustice. So far from being a tyrant or "violent persecutor," Josephus (who was not of the same sect) informs us that he was a ruler of much generosity, who suffered, like his father, from the wrong-doing of others, and he was at length cruelly murdered by a band of ruffians when endeavouring to save the city from an outbreak of lawlessness ("War" iv. v. 2).

But the mixed government and composite state of religion and society, which existed at Jerusalem in the time of Jesus, were a much greater safeguard against persecution than the benevolent disposition of the leading men. In order that priests and rulers should punish people for holding adverse religious views, they must not only be of a bigoted spirit, but members of a completely dominant sect, so as to have behind them the support of a strong public opinion. If the Sadducees had formed an overwhelming orthodox body in Judæa, as the Catholics do in modern Spain, and the nation had been equally independent, they might have been tempted to carry all their measures with a high hand, and show very little respect for the rights and opinions of a minority. We know, however, that their position was exactly the reverse of this; they were confronted by rivals more numerous than themselves, and were at the same time held in check by a strong foreign secular Power, so that any exercise of tyranny on their part was not to be thought of, and if Torquemada had occupied the place of the liberal high-priest, Annas, he could not have been a persecutor.

The Romans are known to have been very severe in dealing with insurrection or sedition; but they were just as tolerant of creeds and forms of worship as the English rulers are at the present day in India. They not only refrained from interfering with any sect so long as it practised no obscene rites and was believed to be loyal to their government, but they everywhere compelled rival sects to respect one another. Gibbon affirms that there cannot be discovered any trace of Roman intolerance towards the professors of Christianity previous to the cruelties that were perpetrated on those who were falsely accused of incendiarism in the time of Nero. Dean Milman shows that the sudden and fitful outbreak of violence on that occasion was not directed against the Christian religion.

"The Neronian persecution was an accident arising out of the fire at Rome, no part of a systematic plan for the suppression of foreign religions. It might have fallen on any other sect or body of men, who might have been designated as victims, to appease the popular resentment. The provincial administrations would be actuated by the same principles as the central government, and be alike indifferent to the quiet progress of opinions, however dangerous to the existing order of things. Unless some breach of the public peace demanded their interference, they would rarely put forth their power; and, content with the maintenance of order, the regular collection of the revenue, the more rapacious with the punctual payment of their own exactions, the more enlightened with the improvement and embellishment of the cities under their charge, they would look on the rise and propagation of a new religion with no more concern than that of a new philosophical sect, particularly in the eastern part of the empire, where the religions were, in general, more foreign to the character of the Greek and Roman polytheism " (" History of Christianity," Vol. II., p. 4).

Seeing thus the principles on which the government of the Roman empire was conducted in the time of Jesus, every impartial student of history must be convinced that the astounding charges of religious intolerance made by New Testament writers cannot possibly be true. The author of Acts tells us that "there was a great persecution against the Church"; that "Saul made havoc of the Church, entering into every house, and haling men and women, committed them to prison"; that "Saul, breathing out threatenings and slaughter against the disciples of the Lord, went unto the high-priest and desired of him letters to Damascus to the synagogues, that if he found any of this way, whether they were men or women, he might bring them bound to Jerusalem" (Acts vi. 1-3; ix. 1-2). That the high-priest, circumstanced as he was, should thus play the part of a mediæval pope, and that Saul should go about from one Roman province to another, as a grand inquisitor, arresting and punishing people for their religious opinions, is about as extravagant a notion as could well be conceived. Assuming that the writer's account is not purely mythical, we may be quite sure that he is either reporting a mock assault on the brethren designed to attract sympathy, or that what he calls "a great persecution," means that certain Jews took legal proceedings against the

Communistic Church to recover the property of their relatives which, they would say, had been got from them unfairly by the raising of a false alarm.

§ 3.—*Character of the Accusers.*

As it is extremely difficult to believe that the Jewish authorities in the time of Jesus could start a cruel religious persecution, and accomplish atrocious murders, considering their high moral standing, together with their dependent condition; is it more likely that their unlearned and irresponsible accusers, whose testimony has come down to us unsupported, would be guilty of calumny? All well-informed and unprejudiced people must feel constrained to answer in the affirmative; for calumny was, unfortunately, a notorious failing of Christian writers for many centuries. Whatever their virtues might have amounted to in other respects, and however sincere their piety, they could not be induced by any consideration to speak fairly and charitably of their opponents. And they do not appear to have had the least idea of accurate reporting; they neither kept their imagination in check, nor sifted popular rumours which happened to accord with their prejudices, nor entertained any real love of historical truth. It was also easy for an obscure chronicler to disseminate falsehood by the slow mode of publication which formerly existed without being promptly detected and called to account. What he wrote as a partisan calumny, would perhaps not come under the observation of a critical reader who regarded it with distrust till a hundred or two hundred years afterwards. And then, the whole generation concerned in the charge having clean passed away, it might be too late to obtain the evidence that was needed for its complete refutation. Dean Stanley in his

"Lecture on the Study of Ecclesiastical History," has the following just remarks:—

"We may still lament that the story of the Lion is so often told only by the Man, that the lives and opinions of heretics can be traced only in the writings of the orthodox, that the clergy have been so often the sole historians of the crimes of the laity. But we shall have learned at least to know that there is another side, even when that side has been torn away or lost. We shall often find some ancient fragment or parchment, like that which vindicates Edwy and Elgiva from the almost unanimous calumny of their monastic enemies. We shall see that in the original biographies of Becket, partial though they be, enough escapes to reveal that he is not the faultless hero represented to us in modern martyrology" ("Eastern Church," p. 55).

This instruction to students of prejudiced ecclesiastical records, though having special reference to the monkish chronicles of mediæval times, applies equally well to the onesided narratives of the primitive Church. The Evangelists were even more credulous than any of the saints of the crusading period, just as illiberal towards their opponents, and quite as much disposed to wrongfully accuse them and blacken their reputation. And they wrote at such a remote time, and under such a safe curtain of obscurity, that there is no prospect whatever of unearthing an ancient document which may serve as a corrective to some of their hostile allegations. We have to judge their testimony, as it is delivered to us, by its own intrinsic merits; and, apart from the animus by which it is inspired, there are plenty of indications which continually betray its untruthfulness.

Among the early Christians, as well as among the Jews, there were both fictionists like Defoe, and mystics like Swedenborg, and the visions which they respectively recorded, as well as the narratives which they wrote, were accepted readily by a large portion of the community as revelations of truth. Some of the Gospels which circulated extensively in the second and third centuries, and were finally condemned as apocryphal, are known to have been the work of fictionists; they were simply pious frauds intended to confer authority on certain sectarian developments. Others were of a higher order, and may reasonably be considered honest productions, although not reliable history. The authors were evidently possessed with a burning desire to know something more of the life and teaching of Jesus than they had hitherto learnt, and as there was then no authoritative document on the subject commanding acceptance in all Churches, and no living witnesses who could be appealed to, they hoped, in each case, to get the biographical material which they needed by direct revelation. They wrote down freely what presented itself to their minds, not as conscious inventors of fiction, but as men believing themselves divinely inspired to make a discovery of forgotten facts. Inspiration at that time was supposed to render people almost omniscient—it enabled them to predict, with confidence, what would happen in the hidden future, and to say with equal assurance what had transpired in the dim uncertain past.

The four canonical Gospels, which have so long been considered Divine revelation, were written nearer to the time when Jesus lived, and may reasonably be expected to contain less of the mythical element than those of later origin, but they are literary productions of precisely the same character. As pseudonymous works were then so much in vogue, the names appended to them are no guarantee of genuineness, and the twelve apostles were probably as little acquainted with letters as any other Jewish peasants. The writers, whoever they were, had learnt something respecting Jesus, perhaps directly from eye-witnesses, and they would add to this freely from their own inventiveness under the notion that they were miraculously inspired. The doctrinal discourses which are put into the mouth of Jesus in the Fourth Gospel, are as little likely to be genuine as any of the numerous speeches which embellish the history of Josephus. The contradictory birth stories prefixed to Matthew and Luke, are as unmistakable creations of fancy as Milton's and Dante's widely different descriptions of Hell, although each writer may have felt well-assured that what he imagined as happening was Divinely revealed. Other portions of their narrative, which are not purely legendary but rather misrepresentations of fact, they might firmly believe to be true. For any mistake of witnesses, or any mendacious report which was started in accordance with their views, they would be likely to accept without investigation, and give it currency as unimpeachable history.

Throughout the whole of Christendom, it used to be thought at one time that whatever the Evangelists said must be accepted, without question, as inspired truth. Such is not the case now. In the most progressive Churches we continually hear it affirmed that these early chroniclers, so far from being divinely illuminated and constrained to write with the strictest accuracy, were really ignorant and prejudiced men, who greatly misunderstood and misrepresented the teaching of Jesus. It is believed that they have recorded some of his genuine doctrines, and added to these largely their own superstitions and conceits, so as to entail on modern reforming Christians a work of close scrutiny and careful discrimination to get at the pristine truth. Professor Graetz, and other Jewish scholars, entertain the same opinion, although it may not be entirely a sound one; they believe that much injustice has been done to the Prophet of Nazareth by his rude, unappreciative biographers. But ignorant and prejudiced men will always be less likely to obscure the merits of their friends and leaders than to misrepresent and malign their opponents. If the Evangelists so incorrectly apprehended their beloved master as to impute to him sentiments which he never held, and language which he never uttered, how much more ready would they be to ascribe imaginary thoughts, words, and acts to the hated Jewish authorities.

Dr. Armitage Robinson, in his lecture on the Gospel of Peter—a production of the second century—says: "Our writer hates the Jews; his whole account is a commentary on the brief sentence of Aristides' Apology, ' He was pierced by the Jews.' " And further on : "The hatred of the writer to the Jews stands in striking contrast to the just and measured terms of our Evangelists." We quite fail to see any striking contrast between the spirit of the earlier and that of the later narratives. It must not be supposed that hatred and vilification of the Jews commenced with Christian writers of the second century; they simply added something as occasion served, and went a little further in the work of flinging dirt than their predecessors. There is exhibited in the literature of that period a very decided tendency to outdo the representations of earlier records; as the Church continually advanced further in idolatry, each succeeding generation of Christians sought to exaggerate, in two directions, the traditions that had been received—they depicted Jesus as more of a Divine being than he was hitherto regarded, and at the same time did their utmost to make the Jews appear more diabolical.

It has often been said that the kernel of Christianity consists in the fulfilment of the two great commandments of the Law—the love of God and the love of our neighbour. In the New Testament are certain texts which set forth these essentials of religion with great force and beauty, but they are, unfortunately, associated with doctrines of a very different character. Many of the early Christians could not possibly love God and humanity, as they were at times sincerely desirous of doing, in consequence of being infected with two prevalent superstitions—Diabolism and the Martyr-spirit—which caused them to hate all who honestly dissented from their views, and to esteem it advantageous to encounter hostility. These mistaken notions had been gaining an increased hold on a large portion of the Jewish population ever since the Babylonian exile, and they had, in some respects, a more mischievous influence than all the preceding idolatry. They tended more than anything else to estrange those who had not the same training, or were unlike in temperament; they hardened and exaggerated human differences; they led to the assortment of mankind not into associated moral grades all moving educationally in one direction, but into two discordant groups—the perfectly good entitled to the joys of paradise, and the entirely bad doomed to everlasting perdition.

If a primitive Christian, imbued with these doctrines, happened to meet with a person in great trouble or distress, he was at once disposed to render the fellow-creature assistance, without any regard to his race or nationality. But he would not persevere in any acts of kindness unless the suffering individual was extremely ignorant, unless his mind was of the nature of a blank sheet on which any story or doctrine might be written. If the object of pity turned out to be a person of some intelligence, holding strong opinions of his own, and inclined to question or dispute what was told him, the good feeling that had been stirred in the saint's breast soon gave way to anger, for every breath of dissent or disbelief was thought to proceed from the Devil. There was supposed to be only one true doctrine in the world, and the slightest controversial check experienced in announcing it, instead of being borne patiently, was generally resented with fierce acrimonious words. Those who conscientiously held other views were not looked upon as brethren of another school entitled to exercise their own judgment in the matter, and having a right to be treated respectfully; they were esteemed agents of the Evil One warring against the Elect, and therefore quite beyond the pale of charitable consideration and love.

We often hear it said of a good Christian man, at the present day, that he has not a single enemy, and it is very natural and reasonable for such to be the case if he holds no high public position. Why should a man have enemies when he is leading a pure life and doing all that he well can to benefit his fellow-creatures? People may not entirely approve of his plans or agree with his opinions, but love him they must. The Evangelists, however, and other primitive Christians of their type, could hardly conceive it possible for a good man to be generally beloved and respected. They thought that the higher moral excellence a person exhibited, the more certain was he to excite enmity and encounter hostility. For in their opinion Satan, the arch-enemy of mankind, was sure to make such a pattern of righteousness the special object of his assaults, and would seek to destroy him, or do all that was possible to corrupt him or counterwork his efforts. And Satan, roaming about the world with his legions of subject spirits, could easily take possession of a certain number of people and make them willing tools to carry out his nefarious designs. Consequently, hostility from such agents was anticipated, and if a person had no enemies to annoy and molest him, it was considered a bad sign in reference to his merits as a saint; it was thought to signify that he was not sufficiently holy to attract Satan's notice. Persecution of some kind or other was esteemed absolutely necessary to the perfection of saintship, and it was confidently believed that the more a man was wronged and ill-treated in the present life, the greater would be his reward in Heaven.

When we thus come to examine the general mental condition of the early Christians, and the illusions and prejudices by which they were influenced, what reliance can be placed on them as witnesses of extraordinary events or of transactions, which all must allow to be extremely improbable? How can their unsupported assertions be expected to prove that men far better educated and more rational than themselves were guilty of preternatural wickedness? A people dominated as they were by the superstition of Diabolism, could not possibly speak with anything like fairness and scrupulousness of their religious opponents. And as persecution was considered necessary for their future spiritual advancement, and a show of wrong-suffering continually attracted popular sympathy, the temptation which they must have felt in time of peace to create imaginary persecutions and conjure up fictitious martyrdoms would be irresistible.

§ 4.—*The Prophet-killing Charges.*

In considering the tremendous charge of crucifying Jesus from pure malevolence, which is advanced against the Jews, it is important to bear in mind that it does not stand alone, it is only one of a long series of diabolical crimes laid at their doors by succeeding generations of Christians. They are said to have killed many prophets previous to his appearance on earth, to have slain several of his followers soon after his own death, and to have tortured and crucified many Christian children in later times. If these anterior and posterior accusations of cruelty can only be substantiated, it must be allowed that they prove the Jewish race to have such a propensity for shedding innocent blood that their guilt in respect to the Calvary transaction cannot be considered incredible. On the other hand, if these charges are seen to be merely the figments of a hostile imagination, the evidence of character will turn so strongly against the accusers and show them to be of so calumnious a disposition that their principal charge will, presumably, be as baseless as the rest. It is quite clear that a people addicted to slandering their religious rivals, both before and after the alleged murder of their leader, would be likely on that very occasion to have no scruple about casting on them a semblance of guilt. Let us, therefore, set character fairly against character as we should do in an ordinary dispute between well-known parties, and judge whether the probability of falsehood on one side, is greater or less than the probability of fiendish cruelty on the other.

The assertions which the Evangelists have put into the mouth of Jesus respecting former generations of prophets, and the treatment which they received from the people, are an entire misrepresentation of the national history. It is made to appear in his discourses, that the prophets were a succession of righteous men delivering messages from Heaven, and that the people, being desperately wicked, refused to give heed to the words which they spoke, and determined to put them to death (Matt. xxi. 35; xxiii. 29-37; Luke xi. 47-51). In reality, the Jewish people were of a mixed character, like the rest of mankind; they consisted of various moral grades, there were always some good, estimable men in the nation ready to listen to wise words, and there were others exactly the reverse. The prophets who appealed to them from time to time were quite as much mixed; they differed in moral worth and differed in sentiment, indeed, every party and sect seems to have had a prophetic mouth-piece to promulgate its views. They all professed to deliver messages from Heaven, but so far from being all in agreement, continually contradicted and denounced one another. Each vaticinator in delivering his message to the people warned them to beware of the falsehoods of others. "The prophets prophesy lies in my name; I sent them not, neither have I commanded them" (Jer. xv. 14). "Woe unto the foolish prophets that follow their own spirit and have seen nothing. O Israel! thy prophets are like the foxes of the desert" (Ezek. xiii. 3, 4). "The prophets shall be ashamed every one of his vision, when he hath prophesied, neither shall he wear a rough garment to deceive. But he shall say, I am no prophet, I am a husbandman, for man taught me to keep cattle from my youth" (Zech. xiii. 4, 5).

With so many opposing oracles in their midst decrying and denouncing one another as impostors, the more sensible and thoughtful Jews might well be excused for regarding all with a considerable amount of distrust. When a prophet spoke to his countrymen as a true sage, and rebuked with superior wisdom the evil tendencies of the times, he could not fail to quicken the national conscience to some extent, and command wide and lasting respect. But one who appeared as a soothsayer, and foretold earthquakes, famines, the destruction of cities, and other terrible calamities that were about to happen, only kindled a great deal of excitement among the more credulous of the population, and cruelly deceived them. The most mischievous class of vaticinators were those who, like Aristobulus of Alexandria, produced forged predictions antedated to give them the appearance of being actually fulfilled up to the time of their pretended discovery. It was a stratagem of that kind on the part of the unknown author of the Book of Daniel, which imposed on the early Christians the belief in the approaching end of the world. It cannot be said that the Jews erred in slighting these mendacious revelators and refusing to consider the messages they delivered; on the contrary, they gave them a far too ready ear, and the nation, in one way and another, suffered immensely by reason of this credulity. On the whole, it may be affirmed, with far more correctness, that the people were ill-treated by the prophets, than that the prophets experienced injustice at the hands of the people.

There could scarcely be a more calumnious representation than that of the Evangelists in depicting their countrymen as an evil-minded and murderous race, eager to assail Divine messengers. In the previous history of the nation, they could not have pointed to a single recorded instance of a prophet being killed in a time of profound peace from pure love of wickedness. It was only in periods of trouble, when a fierce war of factions existed, that prophets, along with other people, occasionally fell victims to the sanguinary strife. Previous to the Chaldean exile, the Jews were religiously divided in much the same way that the English were divided in Tudor times, and the opposing sects were animated by a like spirit of intolerance. Some of the people were strongly attached to Gentile forms of worship, while others regarded images and all Gentile customs as idolatry, and each party when it managed to get the upper hand persecuted the other. Jezebel, the wife of Ahab, had certain prophets slain who protested against the worship which she introduced from her native country. Elijah and other reformers afterwards slew the prophets of Baal (1 Kings xviii. 40). Such cruelty provoked further retaliation, so that Puritan prophets occasionally met with the same fate as when Zechariah, the son of Jehoida, was stoned at the command of King Joash (2 Chron. xxiv. 21).

In Judæa, as well as in other countries, prophets, when they became political partisans, were liable to be ill-treated during the excitement of war by those who considered them dangerous enemies. What they predicted in favour of one party and against another frequently produced such an impression on the popular mind as to insure the prediction's fulfilment. When, for instance, a prophet of good reputation declared that a city would be captured, or that a king would be overthrown, it was pretty sure to cause discouragement and perhaps defection among those who were desirous to avert such an eventuality. The more stout-hearted would then entreat some other prophet to contradict what he had spoken, or would otherwise clamour for his death. The princes of Judah spoke to their king concerning Jeremiah. "We beseech thee let this man be put to death, for thus he weakeneth the hands of the men of war that remain in the city, and the hands of all the people in speaking such words to them" (Jer. xxxviii. 4).

Such cases of punishing unfriendly prophets in time of war were common enough both among Jews and Gentiles, and there was generally as much wrong committed on one side as there was on the other. A prophet would occasionally be assaulted by an adverse mob, just as our political orators are sometimes treated during the excitement of a fiercely contested election. He had nothing to fear, however, if he set himself above the low considerations of partisan strife, and simply rebuked, as a moral reformer, the vices and evil tendencies of the age.

There is no authentic instance of a Jewish teacher giving such wholesome admonition to his countrymen, as that imparted by the wise Son of Sirach, and being persecuted by them in consequence. The most brutal of the populace would not have presumed to exercise violence towards a sage of that high character, much less would the Sanhedrin have entertained the idea of passing condemnation on him, and putting him to an ignominious death.

A sect so ready to calumniate former generations of Jews in respect to their treatment of prophets, would not be likely to speak with more fairness and truthfulness of those who were then living. The unbelief of the Temple magistracy and most other educated Jews in the approaching end of the world, which the Nazarenes predicted, was considered by the latter an offence of such magnitude as to carry with it every conceivable wickedness. In the fierce diatribe against them which is put into the mouth of Jesus, they are not convicted of killing or even persecuting a single prophet, but oratory exerts itself to the utmost to make them enormously guilty in appearance. So little sense of judicial fairness is manifested towards them that they are not only held responsible for the sins of their fathers, but an attempt is made to heap on their doomed heads the guilt of all the preceding blood of the righteous shed from the beginning of the world (Matt. xxiii. 35, 36). Who really composed this intemperate declamation it is impossible to say, but it very correctly represents the general disposition of the Nazarenes to accuse, incriminate, and blacken all who withstood their high claims, and could not be won over to their belief. Such zealots had not the least idea of meeting their religious opponents in a kindly and charitable spirit; those who held other opinions were expected to yield implicitly to their own unbounded arrogance, and they would evidently stick at nothing in the way of calumniating and filling up the cup of that portion of the community which had rejected their Messianic message.

§ 5.—*Mythical Saint-slaying.*

We are told that many of the companions of Jesus, as well as the prophets who preceded him, were unjustly put to death from a spirit of diabolical wickedness. If this can be satisfactorily proved, it will contribute in no small degree to strengthen the belief that his own Crucifixion was a monstrous crime. But if it turns out that the cruel war said to have been carried on against the saints, is just as much a creation of fancy as the earlier persecutions directed against the prophets, the whole of the Evangelical testimony in respect to the shedding of righteous blood will have a proportionately diminished credibility.

The first of the companions of Jesus that take rank as Christian martyrs are the infant children of Bethlehem, said to have been massacred at the order of Herod the Great. All the most able and unprejudiced Christian scholars are now accustomed to treat this story as a pure myth. The massacre with regard to its purpose—the vain attempt to destroy an infant prodigy destined to accomplish great things—has a striking resemblance to older legends, especially to what Josephus says Pharaoh did after hearing the future greatness of the infant Moses predicted ("Ant." ii. ix. 2). We know that Oriental princes holding an idependent throne have often enough swept dangerous rivals from their path by unscrupulous means; but Herod, a tributary ruler of the Romans, had nothing to fear in respect to the security of his position, excepting removal at their hands for misgovernment. Had the astute Indumean soldier, who had been appointed by the Senate of Rome to rule Judæa, subject to his good behaviour, actually been fool enough to believe that his position was endangered by the birth of some wondrous peasant child, and mad enough, for the chance of removing his supposed rival, to order a sweeping slaughter of young Bethlehemites, those about him would have perceived at once that his mind was disordered, and would not have taken a single step to carry out his extravagant behest. It is quite certain that such a massacre could not have been effected without the consent and aid of a large number of capable men, and how could the king obtain their co-operation and at the same time escape the consequences of his mad misgovernment? We might search through the whole range of human fiction in vain for anything to match the utter imbecility, to say nothing of the monstrous cruelty, of this ill-invented political crime. The author of the legend, and those who first accepted it as an authentic record, must have been in point of intellectual development and knowledge of the world's affairs nothing better than dreaming children.

The next martyrdom which the Evangelists report is that of John the Baptist, who is said to have been beheaded by Herod Antipas the tetrarch of Galilee. There is much less improbability in this charge; we find, too, a corroborative mention of it by the historian Josephus. But the reasons assigned for putting John to death look like fabulous inventions, and there is such an amount of variation in the reports that one might well doubt if they ever had any foundation in fact. It is very unlikely that Antipas, on hearing of the fame of Jesus as a miracle-worker, said to his servants, "This is John the Baptist whom I beheaded; he is risen from the dead." It is still more improbable that he said to the daughter of Herodias on being charmed with her dancing, "Whatsoever thou shalt ask of me I will give it thee, unto the half of my kingdom" (Mark

vi. 23). Had he seriously uttered such extravagant things his sensible friends would have considered him demented, and taken good care that his orders were not carried out. When he married his brother's wife he must have known well that it was contrary to the Mosaic law, and it would have been a monstrous thing to condemn to death John the Baptist, or any of his Jewish subjects, for expressing disapproval of it on that ground. Such an unjust proceeding, so far from silencing those who thought the marriage improper, would have greatly exasperated them and increased their disaffection a hundredfold.

Josephus gives another and equally improbable reason for John's being sentenced to death. "When the people came in crowds to him they were greatly delighted in hearing his words. But Herod was afraid that this great power of persuading men might lead to some sedition, as they seemed ready to do whatever he advised them. So he thought it better to cut John off, and prevent a disturbance, than to let things go on and have to repent for suffering an outbreak to take place. Owing to these apprehensions he was sent as a prisoner to the castle of Macherus, and was there put to death" ("Ant." xviii. v. 2). If John had really very great influence over the people so as to be able to control them with words, any ruler would have been glad to obtain his assistance towards maintaining order, and to imprison and behead such a popular leader when he had done nothing wrong would have been the surest possible means of provoking an insurrection. Assuming, therefore, that John was arrested and condemned to execution by Antipas, it is far more likely to have been on account of disorders actually committed by a portion of his irregular followers than with the view to prevent an anticipated disturbance. There is so much conflicting evidence and uncertainty respecting the fate of the Baptist that it is impossible to say with confidence who was really responsible for the punishment meted out to him, and how far it can be considered unjust. It seems quite clear, however, that the Jewish people, who are stigmatised as inveterate prophet-killers, cannot be charged with rising up against the holy man, and conspiring to put him to death. We are told that they flocked together eagerly to hear his discourses, held him in very high esteem, and were exceedingly grieved at being deprived of his ministrations; such was their usual treatment of prophets.

The first reported martyrdom of a companion of Jesus, after his own Crucifixion, is that of Stephen the Deacon as given in the seventh chapter of Acts. There are several things recorded in this book so manifestly untruthful, that if not legendary, they can only be explained satisfactorily as dramatic illusions. On three different occasions the Apostles are said to have been put in prison, and soon afterwards delivered from their bondage by a miracle (v. 19; xii. 7; xvi. 26). Many people have wondered why John the Baptist was not liberated in the same way, and also the saints who were often incarcerated at a later period in various parts of the Roman Empire. If the angel power that defeated the authorities on these few occasions had only been regularly and consistently employed, it would soon have converted the world. The explanation is, that either these marvellous accounts are mythical, or the Apostles were arrested and subjected to a fictitious imprisonment by secret rulers of their own sect, in order to confirm their faith and stimulate their enthusiasm by an apparently supernatural release. So the stoning of Stephen must have been a mere dramatic display to produce an impression on the credulous, or the report which we have of it is purely legendary; for we know that the Romans maintained religious toleration in Judæa, and would not have permitted a brutal sectarian murder of that kind to be perpetrated with impunity.

We are told that previously to Stephen being brought before the Sanhedrin, Gamaliel, a very influential member of that body, made a speech in reference to the followers of Jesus, but the words put into his mouth cannot possibly be accepted as genuine. If the Sanhedrin had been openly charged with crucifying Jesus, as the writer makes it appear, Gamaliel must have felt greatly concerned at the guilt cast on him and his brother counsellors, and would naturally think of making some statement by way of apology or vindication. He might be expected to say that they were under a serious misapprehension respecting Jesus, or that they were greatly divided, and some of them at least were entirely in favour of his acquittal, or that the responsibility for his death did not attach to them at all. Yet, in the speech imputed to him, there is not the slightest allusion made either to the crucifixion or the resurrection of Jesus, and the Christians are regarded simply as a new religious sect who would prosper if God was with them, but would otherwise soon come to nought (Acts v. 34-38). The strangest thing of all is, that after earnestly entreating the Jews to refrain from molesting this sect, his disciple Saul of Tarsus is represented as persecuting them furiously, and even taking an active part in the alleged stoning of Stephen to death. Either the speech must be a pure invention, or it was made by a pretended Gamaliel. Certainly a personator of the great Jewish ruler played an important part in connection with the martyr Stephen at a subsequent period of Church history.

"In the year 415, in the tenth consulship of Honorius and the sixth of Theodosius the younger, on Friday the third of December, about nine o'clock at night, the venerable priest Lucian was sleeping in his bed in the baptistry where he commonly lay in order to guard the sacred vessels of the church. Being half awake he saw a tall, comely old man of venerable aspect with a long white beard, clothed in a white garment edged with small plates of gold marked with crosses, and holding a golden wand in his hand. This person approached Lucian, and, calling him thrice by name, bade him go to Jerusalem and tell Bishop John to come and open the tombs in which his remains and those of certain other servants of Christ lay, that through their means God might open to many the gates of His clemency. Lucian asked his name. 'I am,' said he, 'Gamaliel, who instructed Paul the Apostle in the Law, and on the east side of the monument lies Stephen, who was stoned by the Jews without the north gate. His body was left exposed there one day and one night, but was not touched by birds or beasts. I exhorted the faithful to carry it off in the night time, which when they had done, I caused it to be carried secretly to my country house where I celebrated his funeral rites forty days, and then caused his body to be laid in my own tomb to the eastward. Nicodemus, who came to Jesus by night, also lies there" (Butler's "Lives of the Saints," Vol. II., p. 183).

The narrative goes on to say that Gamaliel appeared a second and a third time to the priest Lucian, who at length went to Jerusalem and told Bishop John what had been revealed to him respecting the relics. The bishop wept for joy, and desired him to proceed at once and search for them at the place indicated. Lucian called some people together and they commenced searching under a heap of stones near his church. When going next day to that place he was met by a certain monk, Migetius, who declared that Gamaliel had also appeared to him, saying that the relics would be found not there, but at another place called Debatalia. The searchers accordingly went to that spot, and on digging in an old ruinous tomb, soon discovered three coffins, on which were engraved the names of Stephen, Gamaliel, and Nicodemus. There came together to view the precious relics a multitude of people, among whom were several afflicted persons who immediately recovered their health. Much rain also fell at the time, and the country was thus refreshed after a long drought. Avitus, a Spanish priest, obtained a small portion of the relics of St. Stephen, which, on being sent to Minorca, worked astonishing miracles, and effected the conversion of 540 Jews. Other portions were sent to Africa, and not only were many extraordinary cures wrought by them among the churches there, but five persons were raised from the dead. St. Augustine, who has always been considered the most veracious of the Christian Fathers, vouches for the truth of these things (Serm. 323, 324, and De Civ. L. 22, c. viii. s. 21). Protestant writers have severely criticised the great relic discovery at Debatalia, and denied the genuineness, not only of the relics, but of Gamaliel the revelator. Important messages of an authoritative character were frequently delivered in the primitive Church by personation and forgery, and it must be admitted that the narrative forms a very fitting sequel to what is written of Gamaliel and Stephen in the Acts of the Apostles.

The next Christian martyrdom there recorded is that of the Apostle James; we are told that "Herod the king stretched forth his hand to vex certain of the Church, and he killed James the brother of John with with the sword" (Acts xii. 1, 2). This allegation is hard to believe, for a subordinate ruler like Herod Agrippa would not have been permitted to slay the leaders of one Jewish sect just to gratify the spite of their rivals. Moreover, this prince was not at all inclined to intolerance, he was anything but a cruel persecutor. Josephus affirms that he "was mild and equally liberal to all men." On account of his Hellenistic tendencies a certain Jew named Simon accused him of not living strictly according to the Law, so that he ought to be excluded from the Temple. The king, so far from taking offence and putting this man to the sword, invited him to come to the theatre. He then asked his accuser in a low gentle voice, "What is there done in this place contrary to the Law?" Simon could say nothing in reply, but apologised for the accusation which he had made. "So the king, esteeming mildness a better quality than anger, was easily reconciled, and when he had given Simon a small present he courteously dismissed him" ("Ant." xix. vii. 3, 4).

The statement that James was slain in a persecution started by the mild and liberal Herod Agrippa is quite as incredible as the story subsequently promulgated about his brother John being thrown into a cauldron of boiling oil. We have no information to show under what circumstances the report originated or how it was suggested. But in the alleged martyrdom of the other apostle of that name—James the Less—to which reference has been made in § 2, the growth of the legend may be easily traced. Josephus records the stoning of certain law-breakers —evidently robbers from what is mentioned in the context—by command of the Sanhedrin when no Roman procurator was present to authorise such punishment. Some reader of his history in the third or fourth century imagined that the people so stoned must have been Christians, and therefore interpolated the words, "James the brother of Jesus who was called Christ" ("Ant." xx. ix. 1), which soon found general acceptance and now appears in all our modern editions. Hegesippus, a writer of the fourth century who revelled in religious fiction, set to work at improving this imaginary martyrdom. As quoted by Eusebius, he affirms that the Jews carried James up to the battlements of the Temple in order to force him there to make a public renunciation of his faith in Christ. But the apostle took that opportunity to solemnly avow his Christian belief before the assembled multitude. The Scribes and Pharisees, enraged at this testimony, hurled him from the battlements headlong to the ground below in order that he might there be stoned. Though very much bruised and hurt by the fall, he had strength enough to get upon his knees, and in that posture beseech God to pardon his murderers, who knew not what they did. He was assailed by the furious throng with showers of stones, and at length a fuller gave him a violent blow on the head with a club so that he quickly expired (Euseb., l., 2, c. 23).

The martyrdoms of St. Peter and St. Paul at Rome, the former by crucifixion and the latter by the headsman's axe, are purely legendary. According to an ancient Roman tradition, they were both led together out of the city by the Ostian gate and put to death on the same day, the 29th of June. No reliable documentary evidence to that effect has been produced, and it is the general opinion of Protestant investigators that Peter was never at Rome at all. An absurd story is told of his encountering Simon Magus in the city and so foiling that famous magician's attempt to fly as to cause his death. This fatality is said to have greatly provoked Simon's patron, the Emperor Nero, who now resolved that the apostle should suffer in turn. The Christians of Rome therefore entreated him to withdraw for a while and escape the tyrant's vengeance, and he reluctantly yielded to their persuasions. But on going out of one of the city gates in the night-time he met Christ and asked of him, " Lord, whither art thou going?" Christ answered, "I am going to Rome to be crucified again." Peter understood this vision to be a strong reproof of his own cowardice. So he returned to the city and was soon arrested and confined with Paul in the Mamertine prison. The two apostles there engaged so earnestly and successfully in prayer as to convert the captains of the guard and forty-seven others, but they were at length scourged and led forth to martyrdom (Butler's "Lives of the Saints," Vol. I., pp. 863, 878).

The martyrdom at Alexandria of St. Mark, who is said to have been the associate and assistant of St. Peter, is thus recorded: "He encouraged the faithful and again withdrew, the "Oriental Chronicle" says, to Rome. On his return to Alexandria the heathens called him a magician on account of his miracles, and resolved upon his death. God, however, long concealed him from them. At last, on the Pagan feast of the idol Serapis, some that were employed to discover the holy man, found him offering to God the prayer of the oblation or the mass. Overjoyed to find him in their power, they seized him, tied his feet with cords, and dragged him about the streets, crying out that the ox must be led to Bucoles, a place near the sea, full of rocks and precipices, where oxen were probably fed. This happened on Sunday, the 24th of April, in the year of Christ 68, of Nero the 14th, about three years after the death of SS. Peter and Paul. The saint was thus dragged the whole day, staining the stones with his blood, and leaving the ground strewed with pieces of his flesh; all the while he ceased not to praise and thank God for his sufferings. At night he was thrown into prison, in which God comforted him with two visions, which Bede has also mentioned in his "True Martyrology." The next day the infidels dragged him as before till he happily expired on

25th of April, on which day the Oriental and Western Churches keep his festival" (*Ibid.*, p. 517).

All the parade of Apostolic martyrdom presented to us by the ecclesiastical writers is clearly just as much founded on imagination as the various cruel torments exhibited in Dante's "Inferno." It was thought by the chroniclers of the fourth century that James, Peter, Andrew, and the rest, would be sure to fall victims in some way or other to the malice of their enemies, and there were consequently invented for them glorious and befitting deaths. We have no reason to believe that a single companion of Jesus was violently deprived of life, with the exception of John the Baptist, and he was not imprisoned and executed on account of his religion. Milman, who is disposed to place implicit reliance in the unveracious statements of the Book of Acts, has the following remarks in reference to the supplementary legends which were produced at a later period:—

"Christian gratitude and reverence soon began to be discontented with the silence of the authentic writings as to the fate of the twelve chosen companions of Christ. It began first with some modest respect for truth, but soon with bold defiance of probability to brighten their obscure course till each might be traced by the blaze of miracle into remote regions of the world where it is clear that if they had penetrated at all no record of their existence would be likely to survive. These religious invaders, according to the later Christian romance, made a regular partition of the world and assigned to each the conquest of his particular province. Thrace, Scythia, Spain, Britain, Ethiopia, the extreme parts of Africa, India—the name of which mysterious region was sometimes assigned to the southern coast of Arabia—had each its apostle whose spiritual triumphs and cruel martyrdom were vividly portrayed and gradually amplified by the fertile invention of the Greek and Syrian historians of the early Church " (" History of Christianity," Vol. II., p. 13).

§ 6.—*The Crucified Children.*

We will now proceed to investigate another series of alleged martyrdoms, which, according as they stand or fall, will intensify the Jewish character for fiendish atrocity, or that of the Christians for untruthfulness. The first recorded persecutions that fell on the Church are evidently fictitious, but from the reign of Nero to the reign of Diocletian, the Christians were really persecuted occasionally in various parts of the Roman Empire, and the reasons for their being subjected to such treatment are perfectly intelligible. They were not tolerated because of their own intolerance; it was plainly seen that they intended to permit no form of worship to exist, but that which they promulgated themselves. They were looked upon as an invading host, fighting insidiously, not with their hands, but with their tongues, for the complete overthrow of Cæsar's dominion and the subversion of the established system of religion. Their secret nocturnal meetings, their refusal, for a long while, to serve in the army, the frequent disturbances which arose from their teaching, and the prophecies which some of them delivered respecting the impending destruction of Rome, all contributed to make them appear a dangerous revolutionary sect in the eyes of Roman magistrates.

The Pagans believed that unless sacrifices were regularly offered, the gods would afflict their land with storms, famine, pestilence, and all sorts of calamities. The Christians, on the other hand, felt assured that if they conformed to the custom of offering sacrifices, the wrath of Heaven would be upon them, and they would suffer everlastingly in hell-fire. Separation, as in the case of Abraham's people and those of Lot, was the wise and proper course under such circumstances for the avoidance of strife. It was inevitable that a conflict of obstinate superstitions should lead to some violence, and the judicial shedding of blood. And in the martyrologies of the Church we do not get anything like a fair and impartial account of the provocation which was given, and the wrong which was perpetrated on the one side and on the other. It is there made to appear that the Pagans alone were culpable, that the one great aim of their magistrates was not to repress evil-doers, but to worry the righteous with fiendish malignity, and sweep them from the face of the earth. This belief served to stimulate and justify the intolerance which the Christians showed in their persistent propagandism. Being assured that evil spirits infested all the temples, that Satan was doing everything in his power to persecute and destroy them, they felt that there could be no peace and security for them till they had completely overthrown Satan's dominion, or in other words, had clean exterminated every doctrine and form of worship that differed from their own.

During the long and fierce struggle which the conquering Church had with Paganism, Christians were seldom brought into contact with Jews, and comparatively little notice was taken of the now weak dispersed people who had been their earliest religious opponents. But when Paganism was at length completely crushed throughout Europe, when every temple was destroyed, and the small synagogue congregations alone refused to accept Christian teaching, these obstinate unbelievers could not fail to attract more attention, and draw upon themselves increased hostility. At the season of Easter, fanatical monks were accustomed to dilate on the terrible blackness and malignity of the Jewish character, as portrayed by the Evangelists. While Jesus went about conferring inestimable benefits on his countrymen, bringing down blessings from Heaven upon them, and ought to have been loved exceedingly, the Devil, always on the watch to accomplish some great mischief, instigated them to put him to death. But some of that accursed race still existed among them, and were hardened, impenitent, and unbelieving as ever, thus approving of their ancestors' evil deeds. They were just as much under the influence of the Devil as the chief priests and rulers were; they hated Christ as much, and were doubtless longing continually to crucify him afresh, as they certainly would seek to do if he were then to reappear on earth. Such was the belief regularly instilled into the Christian multitude during Passion Week, and it cannot be a matter of surprise that calumnious stories should have been told in accordance with it, and that evidences of vicarious crucifixion, should have been fabricated at certain places to afford it the strongest possible confirmation.

The cry of martyrdom as a means of attracting popular sympathy has generally been raised by the weak against the strong, especially by a weak struggling revolutionary party against the repressive measures of a strong government. For several centuries the Christians were such a disturbing body in the Roman Empire, constantly at variance with the authorities, and it was then easy enough to depict the magistrates before whom they were occasionally brought as sanguinary oppressors. But when they at length acquired a dominant position themselves, and unbelievers stood in awe of them, it became difficult to present a reasonable appearance of suffering at their hands injustice. If a quarrel arose between Christians and Jews, and violence ensued, the latter were sure to be overpowered and put to flight. If a Christian summoned his Jewish neighbour before the tribunals, he could always depend on the judicial balance being strongly inclined in his favour. Any story, therefore, of the weak and despised people ill-treating opponents who were so well able to take care of themselves, could scarcely obtain credit. The only way in which Jews in their then humbled condition could be expected to exercise a supposed propensity to shed innocent blood was, by falling on Christian children who happened to stray in their vicinity and putting them to death. Accordingly, the popular imagination turned in this direction in endeavouring to fasten on them charges of guilt; not being able to oppress men like the wicked rulers in Christ's time, it was thought that they would be sure to take advantage of every opportunity afforded them to wreak their vengeance on helpless children.

The numerous child martyrdoms ascribed to Jewish malignity during the Middle Ages are frequently treated by modern writers as pure fictions: it is represented that they were extravagant myths of that period which got to be accepted at length as authentic narratives. This is a mistaken view; the stories were not such fables as those that were written respecting the apostles and the children of Bethlehem; they invariably originated from a basis of fact, that is, from fabricated evidences of murder. The body of a child was occasionally found nailed up to a tree or a wall, but oftener on the ground, and wounded in such a way as to suggest that it had recently been crucified. Suspicion was therefore instantly directed against the Jews, as it was thought that they alone were capable of committing such hellish deeds. They were never caught red-handed in the murderous acts imputed to them, but from the mere finding of a wounded body in their vicinity, their guilt was inferred. Consequently they were arrested and put on trial, some of their number were perhaps tortured into a confession, or one having a quarrel with his kindred, would turn Christian and falsely accuse them. Under the most favourable circumstances they had no chance of establishing their innocence in the face of the strong prejudice directed against them, and they were speedily condemned to a cruel death. Then there were people who would profit by the cancelling of debts due to them, or by the forfeiture of their goods, while the Church gained considerably by enshrining the relics of the child-martyr, which soon wrought a succession of miraculous cures, and attracted crowds of pious people in a commemorative pilgrimage. In the long calendar of Christian saints preserved with so much veneration by the Roman Catholic Church, we find under the date of March 24th, mention of the two following, who are said to have fallen victims to the diabolical malice of the Jews:—

St. Simon of Trent.—"In the year 1472, when the Jews of Trent met in their synagogue on Tuesday in Holy Week to deliberate on the preparations for the approaching festival of the Passover, which fell that year on the Thursday following, they came to the resolution of sacrificing to their inveterate hatred of the Christian name some Christian infant on the Friday following, or Good Friday. A Jewish physician undertook to procure such an infant for the horrid purpose. And while the Christians were at their office of Tenebræ, on Wednesday evening, he found a child called Simon, about two years old, whom, by caresses and by showing him a piece of money, he decoyed from the door of a house—the master and mistress whereof were gone to church—and carried him off. On Thursday evening the principal Jews shut themselves up in a chamber adjoining to their synagogue, and at midnight began their cruel butchery of this innocent victim. Having stopped his mouth with an apron to prevent his crying out, they made several incisions in his body, gathering his blood in a basin. Some, all this while held his arms stretched out in the form of a cross, others held his legs. The child being half dead, they raised him on his feet, and while two of them held him by the arms, the rest pierced his body on all sides with their awls and bodkins. When they saw the child had expired they sung round it: 'In the same manner did we treat Jesus, the God of the Christians; thus may our enemies be confounded for ever.' The magistrates and parents making strict search after the lost child, the Jews hid it first in a barn of hay, then in a cellar, and at last threw it into the river. But God confounded all their endeavours to prevent the discovery of the fact, which being fully proved upon them with its several circumstances, they were put to death, the principal actors in the tragedy being broken upon the wheel and burnt. The synagogue was destroyed, and a chapel was erected upon the spot where the child was martyred. God honoured this innocent victim with many miracles."

St. William of Norwich.—"This martyr was another victim of the implacable rage of the Jews against our holy religion. He suffered in the twelfth year of his age. Having been not long bound an apprentice to a tanner in Norwich, a little before Easter in 1137, the Jews of that city having enticed him into their houses, seized and gagged him; then they bound, mocked, and crucified him in derision of Christ; they also pierced his left side. On Easter-day they put the body into a sack and carried it into Thorp Wood, now a heath, near the gates of the city, there to bury it, but being discovered, left it hanging on a tree. The body was honoured with miracles, and in 1144 removed into the churchyard of the Cathedral of the Holy Trinity by the monks of that abbey, and in 1150 into the choir. On the place in Thorp Wood, where the body of the martyred child was found, a chapel was built, called St. William in the Wood. Mr. Weaver writes that 'the Jews in the principal cities of the kingdom did use sometimes to steal away, circumcise, crown with thorns, whip, torture, and crucify some neighbour's male child in mockery and scorn of our Lord and Saviour Jesus Christ.' St. Richard of Pontoise, in France, was martyred by them in that manner. As also St. Hugh, a child crucified at Lincoln in 1255" (Butler's "Lives of the Saints," Vol. I., p. 391).

With respect to the first mentioned child-martyr, St. Simon of Trent, Professor Graetz, writing in behalf of the Jewish community, declares that the boy was accidentally drowned in the river Etsch. His body, floating down the stream, was caught in a grating, and on its being discovered suspicion was at once directed against the Jews as having probably murdered him. The Bishop of Trent encouraged the popular belief, and several Jews of the city were arrested, imprisoned, and subjected to severe tortures in order to force from them a confession. Then one of their own race appeared as a witness against them, and his testimony was thought to establish their guilt beyond all doubt. A baptised Jew, one Wolflan, from Ratisbon, an engrosser, came forward with the most fearful accusations against his former co-religionists. His charges found the more credence from the fact that the imprisoned Jews confessed under torture that they had slain Simon and drunk his blood on the Passover. The result was that all Jews were banished from Trent, and it was decided that none should thenceforth settle in the city. Four persons only became converts to Christianity and were pardoned. The Bishop of Trent and the monks made every effort to utilise this circumstance so as to achieve the general ruin of the Jews. The body of the child was embalmed and commended to the populace as a holy relic. Thousands made pilgrimages to its remains, and ere long it was believed by some that they saw the bones of the child glitter. From every chancel the Dominicans proclaimed the new miracle, and thundered against the infamy of the Jews. Two lawyers from Padua, who visited Trent to convince themselves of the truth of the occurrence, were almost torn to pieces by the fanatical mob. The marvel gradually came to be believed in, and so the Jews in all Christian countries were jeopardised anew. Even in Italy they dared not go outside the towns lest they should be slain by the first comer as child-murderers" ("History of the Jews," Vol. IV., p. 320).

Mr. Joseph Jacobs, in a recent paper read before the Jewish Historical Society, has shown that the martyrdom of little St. Hugh, of Lincoln, as recorded by Matthew Paris, rests on very similar evidence. The child had in all probability died from accidental drowning, and on its body being found it was supposed to have fallen a victim to Jewish malice. One suspected Jew, named Jopin, to save himself, was frightened into making a confession, which consisted of the most extravagant accusations against his brethren, implicating all the principal Jews of England. Many were therefore tried, condemned, and executed, and Jopin at length met with the same fate, though such as he generally escaped by submitting to baptism. There were always a few irreligious and unprincipled Jews ready to turn Christian, Mahommedan, or anything else to escape persecution, or to gain some slight pecuniary advantage. The horrifying testimony of such mean knaves was considered worthy of belief because it entirely accorded with the prevalent Anti-Jewish prejudice, while that of their honest brethren, from its being contrary to popular expectations and wishes, was scornfully rejected. The accused who conscientiously told the truth were speedily got rid of at the gallows or the stake, while those who spoke falsely and brought them to this unjust doom, were left to propagate their lies without fear of contradiction.

Dr. Jessop had recently an interesting article in *The Nineteenth Century* on the martyrdom of St. William of Norwich, as reported by the monk Thomas of Monmouth. The whole case, as he clearly shows, originated from extreme credulity and Anti-Jewish prejudice, coupled with a desire on the part of some to dispossess the Jews of their wealth. He is not warranted, however, in assuming that the first instance of child-martyrdom is that of the boy tied up and flogged to death by some Jews at Inmestar in the year 430, as recorded by the ecclesiastical historian Socrates. For the youth so cruelly punished was not made a saint of, and the violence to which he was subjected was in no sense a diabolical crime. It was simply an act of retaliation on the part of the Jews against one of a mob of Christians who interrupted them while celebrating the Feast of Purim. Similar cases of fatal violence occur now and then in India at the present day, when conflicts arise between excited Hindoos and Mussulmans at their festival seasons. The mediæval outrages ascribed to the Jews were of a distinctly Satanic character. They were supposed to kidnap and murder children who fell in their way without any provocation at all, and simply to gratify their inveterate hatred of Christ. So rooted was this belief that in the severe penal laws enacted against the Jews of England in the reign of Edward I. (a few years before their expulsion), one clause insisted on their not stirring from their habitations on Good Friday, when they were thought to be especially dangerous.

In consequence of the terrible charges brought against them, the Jews were at length banished from this country in 1290, and their exclusion was maintained for nearly four hundred years. They were afterwards expelled from France, and at a still later period from Spain and Portugal, under circumstances of great cruelty. Meanwhile the Reformation, which was making steady progress throughout Northern and Central Europe, turned in no small measure to their advantage. The reforming teachers protested against the worship of saints and their relics as a gross idolatry, and St. William of Norwich and the numerous other alleged victims of Jewish malice obtained no more favourable consideration at their hands than St. Thomas of Canterbury. Discredit was thrown on the miracles wrought at the various holy shrines, and the number of wonderful cures would be sure to decrease with the gradual cooling down of the excitement from which they originated. Fewer people, from year to year, attended the once crowded pilgrimages, and they were at length abandoned altogether as being in the eyes of reformed Christians without use and without merit. Under these circumstances, martyr-making was a ruined business, there was no longer any inducement for enterprising priests to get hold of the bodies of children supposed to have been crucified and establish new shrines, even if they found for that purpose a favourable opportunity.

Another Reformation doctrine that mitigated the prejudice against the poor worried Jews was the rejection of the Roman Catholic tenet of Transubstantiation. As long as Christ was supposed to be really present in the consecrated wafer, that emblem was of course believed to be endowed with life; if wounded it must suffer pain and bleed as his body had done when it hung on the cross. Hence the imagined eagerness of the Jews to assault the Host on Good Friday and the miraculous results which followed, of which fictitious traces calculated to incriminate them were occasionally found. They were thought to be simply perpetrating afresh the diabolical cruelty of their ancestors and exulting in the Redeemer's humiliation and sufferings. When, however, the opinion began to prevail that the bread or wafer after consecration was not transubstantiated into the body of Christ, but continued of the same nature as before, it was felt that there could be no sense or reason in treating it as a thing of life. The Jews would surely not break into churches at the risk of being subjected to torture and condemned to the severest death penalty just for the purpose of stabbing a representative substance which could be equally well done in the privacy of their own homes. And as to the stories of the Host being found bleeding from their assaults, they must have originated from false appearances, and, like many other marvels of the Roman Church, were to a reasonable Christian wholly unworthy of belief.

The two great charges advanced against the Jews in mediæval times of attacking Christ vicariously were thus weakened and invalidated to a considerable extent by the more enlightened Christian teaching. But Luther and many other Reformers continued as hostile as the Romanists had been towards the long-suffering people. Nor was the voice of calumny, which persistently followed them, by any means silenced, it only modified its assertions to some extent with the change in the popular belief. They were now generally charged with poisoning wells, practising sorcery, and of murdering any Christian who opportunely fell in their way for the purpose of mixing his blood in their Passover cakes. In vain they protested that such a ritualistic abomination was not sanctioned by either Bible or Talmud, and that it was altogether contrary to the principles of their religion. The accusation was repeatedly brought against them at Easter time, and without being allowed the slightest chance to clear themselves, they were imprisoned, tortured, sometimes into a mad confession, convicted, and finally burnt to death. As in the case of the child-crucifixions, it was easy enough to procure a dead body and place it in a wounded condition near to their dwellings so as to create a suspicion of its having fallen a victim to their violence. Their great champion, Manasseh Ben Israel, who, at the end of the seventeenth century, assisted their return to England, complains of this incriminating stratagem being frequently resorted to in his time; and it has been practised occasionally in the present century in countries where the Greek Church is dominant and much ignorance exists, though generally with no worse results than the exciting of a brutal mob against the Jews and their being subjected to a period of unjust imprisonment.

Protestant missionaries, who still labour for the conversion of the Jews, generally endeavour to make a sort of compromise with them in respect to the numerous charges of diabolism which have been advanced against their race. If the Jews will only admit the truth of the first great accusation coming from the Evangelists, the missionaries on their part will acknowledge that all which have since followed from century to century have been an unbroken series of calumnies. But no really enlightened Jew can be expected to make such an admission, for in his eyes the persistent untruthfulness of the later and better instructed accusers must necessarily weaken the credit of their predecessors. And he will not have been trained to consider the Gospel of Matthew a more holy and trustworthy document than the narrative of good, devout Matthew Paris. If it is clearly proved that a certain individual Christian was extremely untruthful during the whole period of his youth and early manhood, not much reliance will be placed in any extraordinary testimony which he may have delivered when merely a child. So it cannot be supposed that the Christian community, which has made such great intellectual and moral progress, was in its primitive state entirely free from any disposition to blacken and defame the Jews who rejected its message, when it is undeniable that for several hundred years afterwards it systematically slandered and sought to incriminate their posterity.

If the Jews during the Middle Ages had been looked upon as ordinary human beings, and there had been no previous charge of Satanic crime against them universally accepted on the authority of the Evangelists, the absurd stories of their insulting the consecrated Host and crucifying children in hatred of Christ would not have obtained credit for a moment. It would have occurred to everybody that a shrewd, calculating race would be very unlikely to perpetrate outrages which must necessarily excite the popular vengeance against them, and could not contribute in the slightest degree to their advantage, even if there were no risk of detection and punishment. The monstrous deeds imputed to them are now universally discredited by sensible people, just as the witchcraft crimes of that period are no longer believed, because the notion of the Devil getting hold of people and inducing them to renounce all their human sympathies and risk their lives as his agents of wickedness is well known to be a delusion. But when this superstition is once surrendered it must be clear to every unprejudiced mind that there is no better ground for believing the Satanic atrocities of the first century. The astounding charges of bloodguiltiness started against the Jews by the primitive Church, are not supported by any stronger testimony than the kindred accusations subsequently advanced by the mediæval Church, and the whole of the monstrous allegations of devilry must stand or fall together.

We sometimes hear it said that the Jews who were accused of preternatural wickedness during the Middle Ages never had anything like a fair trial. Few would think of denying this, but the Jewish rulers who were long before impeached by the Evangelists had no trial at all; an opportunity was never given them to say anything in the way of defence before an impartial tribunal, for the written charges against them were only made at a safe distance behind their backs or after they were silent in their graves. They may possibly have heard of a report being circulated that they had wickedly plotted against Jesus and delivered him up to be crucified, but in such case they must have considered it an idle story, unworthy of serious refutation. There is no evidence to show that the Evangelists were less credulous or less prejudiced than the monkish chroniclers of a later period. The Rev. Dr. M'Caul, in an able refutation of the mediæval charges, contends that one good reason for disbelieving them is their being accompanied by so many "lying wonders." This is a very sensible judgment, but are we to consider the gospel miracles veracious wonders when they equally contradict the ordinary experience of mankind? It cannot be made out that the earlier accusations are in any degree less outrageous in character than those made long afterwards; they are, if possible, to some extent even more so. The Jews would be very unlikely at any period to murder an innocent child that had done them no harm, yet they might be sooner expected to commit such a senseless crime than crucify a generous friend who stood ready to heal their ailments and would presumably, if his life were prolonged, confer on them an incalculable amount of good. In the earlier and the later charges alike reasonable human conduct seems to be entirely lost sight of, as though it had no existence on earth, and enormous cruelty is continually associated with unparalleled imbecility.

§ 7.—*No Motives for Murder.*

In balancing the character of the accusers against that of the accused and examining the successive charges of bloodguiltiness advanced against the, latter we have more than once in the preceding sections affirmed that they could have no real motive for putting Jesus to death. It will be well now to direct further attention to this point, for very much importance is rightly attached to the question of motive in all criminal investigations. An individual will now and then commit a murder from insanity or from some sudden fit of passion or caprice which it is hard to explain, but where a number of people band themselves together to take life it is invariably done on rational grounds. Associated murderers think well on what they are about, they resolve to shed blood as a matter of policy with the view to gain some prospective advantage, just as a nation does when it makes a declaration of war. The Jewish rulers were a body of men accustomed to deliberate, constantly occupied in discussing public affairs, and very unlikely to act precipitately; and we may be sure that they would not have decided in full council on killing the prophet of Nazareth unless some overpowering reason had urged them on to such a course. But no strong reason which could have determined them to perpetrate an offence of so much gravity has ever yet been made known to the world.

Other motives than mere devilishness have been suggested from time to time to account for the deadly hostility said to have been directed against Jesus by his unbelieving countrymen. At his trial, or rather mock trial, it is very probable that a number of unreasonable charges were brought against him in order to make it appear that his opponents were animated by pure malignity and were unable to cast on him any serious reproach. But one charge which the Evangelists mention, that of blasphemy, could hardly have suggested itself even to a mock tribunal, and it is very probably a later mythical invention. If Pagans occasionally professed to be divine, Jews never thought of doing so, and it is extremely unlikely that a notion so entirely foreign to the Mosaic religion ever entered the mind of Jesus. Supposing, however, that he had really believed what his followers came eventually to believe—that he was begotten of his Father before all worlds—he could not have been held guilty of blasphemy in consequence and condemned to death; his countrymen would only have considered him mad. Dr. Benisch writes as follows respecting this absurd accusation:—

"Was he condemned because he called himself the Son of God? Every Judean addressed God as his Father in Heaven. All Israel are called in the Bible 'God's children.' God distinctly called David 'My son.' How, therefore, could a Judean be condemned for an utterance which might have been, and no doubt was, in the mouths of thousands of his countrymen? Surely no one will maintain that when Jesus called himself the Son of God and his disciples assented to that designation, they understood it in a sense subsequently given it by the Council of Nice or in the Apostles' Creed. Of such a sonship the disciples could have no idea. Was it for the crime of constructive blasphemy for which he was condemned? The Jewish penal code knew of no such crime. A blasphemer had to utter distinctly the ineffable name before witnesses and revile it. Such an utterance, and nothing else, constituted blasphemy and brought on the punishment of death" ("Judaism and Christianity," p. 32).

Some writers have endeavoured to make out that Jesus must necessarily have encountered a great deal of hostility from the various Jewish sects. They think that the Sadducees are sure to have been strongly prejudiced against him because he held the doctrine of the resurrection, that the Pharisees would regard him with still greater enmity through his slighting their rigid ceremonialism, and that every other sect would dislike him in consequence of his failing to adopt their peculiar views. But why should he, more than other independent teachers, be hated on every side for failing to place himself in accord with the sects? Had he been seated on the throne of Judæa and universally recognised as sovereign, he could not have been expected to please everybody, or entertain the sentiments of every portion of the community. But he held no high regal position nor had a very large and important following that his countrymen should feel much concerned about what particular doctrines he favoured or despised. His religious sentiments were pretty much of the same character as those of John the Baptist who, so far from exciting general hatred by his public utterances, is said to have been well received by the people in all parts of the country. There was nothing in the teaching of Jesus contrary to a liberal interpretation of the Law, certainly nothing to provoke a feeling of intense animosity which could only be satisfied by his condemnation to an ignominious death.

The New Testament makes it appear that of all the Pharisees who set themselves in opposition to the teaching of Jesus, Saul of Tarsus was the most violent and implacable. But we are not informed of the reasons which this remarkable man had for his hostility to the new sect, and it is a great pity that there were not preserved some of the doctrinal epistles which he wrote previous to his conversion. Did he dislike the communism of the Galilean brotherhood? Perhaps so, as he did not conform to it, but there is no intimation to that effect in any of his extant writings. Was he under the impression that they were not sufficiently strict in keeping the Sabbath, and complying with the various other regulations of the Law? That could hardly have been the ground on which his furious opposition was based, for when he was at length favoured, above all other Pharisees, with a special revelation, and induced to join the Church that he had assailed, he went far beyond Jesus in ceremonial laxity, and considered it unnecessary to keep the Sabbath at all (Col. ii. 16). Dean Milman endeavours to account for the alleged hostility which gathered about Jesus as follows:—

"He appeared as equal, as superior to Moses, as the author of a new revelation which, although it was not to destroy the Law, was in a certain sense to supersede it by the introduction of a new and original faith. Hence the implacable hostility manifested against Jesus not merely by the fierce, the fanatical, the violent, the licentious, by all who might take offence at the purity and gentleness of his precepts, but by the better and more educated among the people—the Scribes, the Lawyers, the Pharisees. Jesus at once assumed a superiority not merely over the teachers of the Law—this acknowledged religious aristocracy, whose reputation, whose interests, and whose pride were deeply pledged to the maintenance of the existing system—but he set himself above those inspired teachers of whom the rabbis were only the interpreters. . . . . He superseded at once, by his simple word, all that they had painfully learned and regularly taught as the eternal and irrepealable word of God, perfect, complete, enduring no addition. Hence their perpetual endeavours to commit Jesus with the multitude as disparaging or infringing the ordinances of Moses; endeavours which were perpetually baffled on his part by his cautious compliance with the more important observances, and notwithstanding the general bearing of his teaching towards the development of a higher and independent doctrine, his uniform respect for the letter as well as the spirit of the Mosaic institutes. But as the strength of the Rabbinical hierarchy lay in the passionate jealousy of the people about the Law, they never abandoned the hope of convicting Jesus on this ground, as a false pretender to the character of the Messiah. At all events, they saw clearly that it was a struggle for the life and death of their authority. Jesus acknowledged as the Christ, the whole fabric of their power and influence fell at once" ("History of Christianity," Vol. I., p. 180).

We are told that the educated Jews, the religious aristocracy who expounded the Law, took great offence at Jesus, because he set himself above all other teachers. It could not possibly have been so. Some years before his time, Hillel, a poor woodcutter, came from Babylon to Jerusalem, and by diligent self-culture, soon surpassed all other men in scholarship, rose to be at the head of the Sanhedrin, and made his voice heard and respected throughout the country as a reformer of the Law. If no great jealousy and apprehension was excited by this upstart teacher attaining pre-eminence, how could Jesus, with a few peasant followers, be expected to call forth such a feeling, when even, after emerging from obscurity, he held no commanding position in the country, and was but very little known? Judas Maccabæus, without any claim to royal blood or regal authority, went so far as to set himself above all other teachers, both modifying the observance of the Law on several occasions, and adding to the sacred books, yet he did not thereby give great offence. The temple magistracy and the rabbins, so far from breathing hostility against him, were ready enough to submit to his leadership, for they saw that he was a capable man, strong enough to move the entire nation. And if Jesus had shown a corresponding power of ruling and directing the people by military or any other means, the educated classes would, with just as little hesitation, have gone over to him and ranged themselves loyally under his command. As he failed to exert any great influence in the country, they would not feel disposed to place their trust in him, they would naturally hold aloof from him and discredit his Messianic claims, but they would have no reason whatever to fear that their position was endangered by his teaching, so that it would be desirable to make open war against him and find some means of putting him to death.

Milman seems to imagine that the Scribes, Lawyers, and Pharisees would anticipate the future development of Christianity in its world-wide expansion and the immense extent to which it would ultimately depart from Judaism and become as it were an independent religion. But how could they be expected to look for this marvellous growth when there was nothing which presented itself to their observation in the least likely to suggest it? Had they only known that the followers of Jesus would in another generation or two entirely free themselves from the Jewish ordinances, discontinue circumcision, change the Sabbath day, no longer observe the great feasts, and begin to prostrate themselves before images and relics after the manner of the Gentiles, they might well have taken alarm at such a complete departure from their standards, and done all in their power to oppose and prevent the impending revolution. From what they beheld of the

Galilean sect, however, the wisest and most prescient men among them would not have imagined that such an immense distortion, as the result of its future proselytism, had been possible. Jesus himself adhered faithfully to the Law, and was less of an innovator in respect to doctrine than his learned contemporary Philo; the fact of his not being a rigid formalist would cause no more offence than was already given by the disciples of Hillel in disputing with the disciples of Shammai. What he continually and emphatically insisted upon in the face of his unbelieving countrymen was the approaching end of the world, and the need of preparing for it by the renunciation of worldly pursuits and pleasures. But this doctrine had been promulgated by other Jewish prophets without provoking hostility, and those who esteemed the announcement false would naturally suppose that after a few years when it was seen to be unfulfilled the Nazarene sect would fall to pieces, just as people in America, fifty years ago, felt confident that the failure of Mormon predictions would result in the speedy break up of that community.

One of the most common theories advanced at the present day to account for the enmity which is supposed to have been directed against Jesus is, that the particular course which he took caused a great national disappointment. We are told that the Jews were led to believe that he would free them from a foreign yoke, that he would pursue a similar policy to that of Gideon, David, Judas Maccabæus, and other national deliverers, and when they saw that he did not act in accordance with their preconceived ideas, but endeavoured in quite a different way to promote their welfare, they were so exceedingly mortified as to determine on taking his life. A more extravagant notion than this could hardly be entertained by any human mind. We know that a community are now and then disappointed in a person who is sent to occupy an established position, and exercise some authority among them; and are consequently led to ask for his removal. The inhabitants of a parish, for instance, may dislike their new vicar for some reason or other, and the population of a colony or province may decry the new governor who comes among them, because he does not act quite in accordance with their wishes. But Jesus had no corresponding relationship to the Jewish people; he was one of several humble aspirants to high authority moving about among them, and was not universally recognised as the legitimate head of the nation. It is quite impossible that his countrymen should have formed any great expectations of him, because the vast majority of them knew nothing at all about him; indeed, it is highly probable that at the time of his death, nine-tenths of them had never so much as heard of his existence. During the greater portion of his career he is said to have followed the profession of a carpenter, and to have lived in complete obscurity at Nazareth. And when he at length commenced his public ministry, he was regarded in much the same light as other itinerant prophets of that period; no intelligent Jew would have supposed that one who went from village to village preaching and working cures was the Heaven-sent national regenerator. There were several prophets and exorcists going about, each with a small following, and so long as they kept within the bounds of the Law, what either of them might do or fail to do for the advancement of his claims would have been to the educated portion of the community a matter of complete indifference. Graetz, the Jewish historian, writing of this period says: "The nation was split into many parties, each entertaining a different idea of the future Saviour, and rendering it therefore impossible that any one aspirant should receive a general recognition as the Messiah."

Jesus lived in peaceable times, when the Roman authority was so firmly and securely established in Palestine that a general rising was quite out of the question, and a fighting Messiah with a handful of followers would only have gained the sympathy of the robber class. All educated Jews would have been glad to see the restoration of their national independence, but as there was not the slightest prospect of such a glorious result being achieved at that period, they thought it best to cultivate friendly relations with the conquerors and make the best of their subordinate position. This was especially the aim of the Temple magistracy; they were anxious to maintain peace and give no countenance whatever to any rash attempt at inciting an outbreak which would be foredoomed to failure. They knew that spasmodic insurrections would not only be repressed with a vigorous hand, but would be certain to entail on the country an increased burden of tribute. Had Jesus, therefore, appeared as a leader of revolt without the slightest chance of effecting a national deliverance, he must necessarily have given great offence to the Jewish authorities, and they might reasonably have desired to effect his removal in the interests of peace. As he refrained from taking a course that was likely to cause a useless effusion of blood, while plenty of dangerous characters existed who might be expected to do so, they would not have pounced upon him as the country's worst troubler, of whom it was especially desirable to make a clean riddance.

The Romans, on whose shoulders the guilt of the Crucifixion is now sometimes cast, could have had no better ground than the Jewish rulers for regarding Jesus as a dangerous opponent, whom it was highly expedient to deprive of life. One who went about with poor, unarmed followers, preaching the doctrine of non-resistance, could not possibly have excited any apprehension in their minds. So long as there was no uprising against the tribute, and no representative of the warlike Asmonean family seeking to restore the Jewish monarchy which Roman arms had suppressed, they would concern themselves little about the claims of a suffering Messiah who, when the end of the world came, was to rule in a Kingdom of Heaven. It was the robbers who gave them continual trouble, the brigand leaders who went from place to place plundering villages, committing murders, and inciting the people to revolt. When one of these fighting heroes fell into their hands they showed him little mercy, and generally proceeded, in the most summary manner, to bring him to execution. The Evangelists, however, would have us believe that a course, strangely at variance with the ordinary Roman policy, was taken by the governor, Pontius Pilate. He had got in safe custody a notorious robber and leader of sedition, whom he was still in no hurry to punish, and was willing, at the base clamour of the Jewish people, to set him at liberty. Nay, to humour the same unreasonable multitude, he was even induced to crucify, by preference, the innocent Jesus, from whom he had nothing whatever to fear. A mock Pilate might have exhibited such outrageous folly and injustice, but the real Pilate would not have done so, he was not a ruler disposed to consult the Jewish people in reference to what course he should take ("Ant." xviii. iii. 1); and he was one of the least likely of procurators to deliberately sacrifice Roman interests for their gratification. Dr. Strauss, who as an able critic does not often err on the side of credulity, in his elaborate mythical theory of expounding the Gospel narrative, has the following remarks on the conduct there imputed to Pilate:—

"That Jesus was put to death by order of the Roman Procurator is certain ('Tacitus Annal,' xv., 44); there is no trace of his having given immediate or personal offence to that officer by his ministry; there is, therefore, every probability in favour of the representation given by our Gospels, that the Jewish authorities, being themselves deprived of the power of life and death by the Romans, endeavoured to gain over the Roman procurator for their purposes, by bringing the man, whom they wished to destroy for hierarchical reasons, into suspicion with the Romans on political grounds. The political character of the Jewish idea of the Messiah made it possible to do this. Jesus had recognised this idea as applicable to himself only hesitatingly, and with a disavowal of its political side; but the people, and even his own disciples had up to that time, taken the less notice of this disavowal in proportion as it was unintelligible to them. So much the more easy was it for the Jewish authorities to represent to Pilate, in a politically dangerous light, the success which Jesus met with in gaining followers among the people, the concourse which attended his lectures, the homage which had been given to him on his entrance into the capital. So far, therefore, the Evangelical narrative has all historical probability in its favour" ("Life of Jesus," Vol. II., p. 356).

So far from it being certain that Jesus was put to death by order of the procurator, it is extremely improbable that Pilate knew anything at all about his trial and crucifixion. We have already shown (page 94) that had he made any report on the subject to the imperial authorities, a document of so much value in the controversy between Pagans and Christians would not have been allowed to perish. Wherever Christians went they propagated their story of the Crucifixion; no one else knew anything about the tragic affair, and it was evidently only through them that the information given by Tacitus would be derived. The Christians were in his eyes an extremely bad set of people, capable of any villainy, although they had been unjustly accused of setting fire to the city, and it would seem to him in every way credible and reasonable that the ringleader of such pestilent wretches should have been caught in his wickedness and sentenced to death by the Roman procurator. But had he known as much as we know about the harmless Galilean sect and their leader, he would have treated the story of his condemnation by Pilate to a punishment which was only inflicted on the worst criminals, as being wholly unworthy of belief.

If Pilate had been so weak-minded as to send an innocent man to execution, simply because a number of malignant people had a spite against him and wanted him put to death, he would have soon found enough to do; there would have been constantly flocking to him a cowardly set who, having quarrelled with some person, and not liking to run the risk of taking his life with their own hands, were determined on getting him crucified. Strauss thinks that the Jewish rulers managed to craftily circumvent Pilate by pretending to be very anxious lest the popularity of Jesus as a religious teacher should lead ultimately to an outbreak, and so cause him great trouble. But would not he have instantly seen through such a flimsy representation advanced to work on his fears, and have known that it was only intended to serve the purpose of a vile sectarian conspiracy? The success of Jesus as a teacher could not possibly cause any apprehension to Roman minds, since his doctrine was favourable to the maintenance of peace; all who went over to him were so many detached from the militant party, who were contemplating, at some future time, an armed resistance.

Jesus had not taken a single step to promote a Messianic revolt, as Rabbi Akiba did in the following century; it was well known that he had no thought of establishing an earthly kingdom or of resorting to force, and for Pilate to condemn to death this leader of a peaceable sect as dangerous, while deeming it quite safe to let loose a captain of brigands to prey on the country, he must have been just such another idiot as Herod the Great is made to appear in the legend of the Babes of Bethlehem.

§ 8.—*Clear Motives for Calumny.*

In modern criminal investigations, when people are accused of murder or any other foul deed, and it is impossible to see how they could be prompted to do it, or expect to gain anything by it, it is usual to ask if the accusers are likely to have any interest in getting up the charge. Had this sound maxim of jurisprudence been regularly acted upon in past times, an immense deal of wrong which has discredited the administration of justice would thereby have been averted. It is clear, for instance, that the Jews during the Middle Ages could have no sane motive for crucifying children and insulting the consecrated Host, there was nothing that they could hope to gain and much that they must necessarily lose by the perpetration of such outrages. On the other hand, their more unscrupulous Christian neighbours were under very strong inducements to get up fictitious evidence against them and render them guilty in appearance. The substantial advantages which they were likely to reap from their condemnation to death and the forfeiture of their property must have been perceptible to the dullest comprehension. And had the absurd charges made against them only been submitted to the consideration of enlightened and impartial judges, the clear indication of their being thus got up from interested motives would at once have insured their acquittal.

It is our purpose now to make it clear that the great charge of crucifying Jesus advanced against the rulers and other educated Jews whom his preaching failed to convince, is quite as ill-founded and in fact of a very similar character. They had no motive whatever for putting him to death, having never been seriously troubled by his humble ministrations; he exercised no dominant power in the land, and it cannot be shown that any party dissenting from his views, or a single individual, would breathe more freely after his disappearance. But though he could be no obstacle in the eyes of the Sanhedrin, that authoritative body must have been considered a tremendous hindrance to the dissemination of his belief, and the establishment of his prospective Kingdom of Heaven. Most thoughtful people, on hearing that the end of the world was announced as imminent, would have expressed themselves as sceptical on the subject because nothing had been said about it by the rulers and other learned men. The enthusiastic propagandists would naturally enough feel vexed at this check which they continually encountered, and would often enough wish that the Jewish authorities were at the bottom of the Dead Sea. As they could not be killed and got rid of, it was desirable in the interests of the Nazarene sect that they should be as far as possible discredited, and there was no practicable way by which this could be accomplished but by calumny. Much might perhaps be done to weaken their influence by accusing them before the people of general wickedness, denouncing them as an evil-minded and murderous generation, eager to shed the blood of the prophets. But the Crucifixion drama performed on the grounds of Joseph of Arimathæa, was an improved method of defamation; in that spectacle their guilt was rendered visible to a number of select witnesses; they were made to appear in the very act of murdering the Messiah. Those who beheld this tragic representation could not fail to be strongly influenced by it; so convinced would they be that the Jewish hierarchy were under the domination of Satan, that no future pleading of the recognised teachers of the Law would ever induce them to respect their authority.

In all countries and in every age there have been men who, though honest and truthful as private citizens, have been thoroughly unscrupulous in the means which they have resorted to for the advancement of a religious or a political cause. At the present day people, as sectarians and partisans, often have recourse to well-contrived fiction for the purpose of calumniating their opponents, as they may thus avoid the risk of being prosecuted for libel. Their bad characters may be meant to represent real personages, although it cannot be proved that they have been introduced with such object. In some instances they are so base and villainous that they are not likely to be recognised by any intelligent reader as mere caricatures. An English newspaper some years ago published a serial story of the sensational type which was designed to exhibit in the worst possible light the Roman Catholic community. The *bête noire* of this slanderous tale, Father Rogier, a priest settled in Wales, was depicted as a swindler, a seducer, a murderer, in short a very monster of wickedness. The more ignorant readers of the journal probably regarded it as a drawing from life, but some few protested against its untruthfulness, and contended that it only exhibited the writer's extreme prejudice and want of Christian charity.

A drama is not so easily and cheaply produced as a tale, but where it is possible to have recourse to such agency, it offers a more effective means of misrepresentation for the purpose of biassing the simple and credulous. The early Methodists were extravagantly vilified by dramatic art, and held up to obloquy and reprobation throughout England. Their preachers were exhibited as the basest hypocrites, wearing a cloak of religion only that they might better overreach people, and more readily gain access to houses for the purpose of seducing weak-minded women. The well-informed and liberal-minded knew that this representation was extremely unjust, and denounced it as such; but it served for awhile to create a strong prejudice against Methodism in nearly all ranks of English society. Many other causes, both political and religious, have, by a similar dramatic perversion on the part of their opponents, been injured to some extent in public estimation, and had attached to them an opprobrium which was wholly undeserved.

In these days of universal culture people cannot be imposed upon by romantic and dramatic art so completely as they often were in a ruder age. The simplest servant girl may be heard to say, now and then, in reference to what she has read or seen, " It is only a tale, you know," or " It is only a play." But in primitive times, when the trickery of tales and plays was unknown and unsuspected, the great mass of mankind were in consequence much more easily misled by such representations of life. The works of the early Jewish fictionists were readily accepted as narratives of fact, and no one was disposed to entertain a shadow of doubt as to their complete accuracy. A people unaccustomed to dramatic art would be just as easily misled in this or that direction by theatrical illusions artfully contrived for the purpose. It was possible to make a select number of the more credulous believe that men in authority, when skilfully personated, stood before them in very deed, and that a foul transaction thus exhibited was the actual perpetration of a crime. And they would go forth as faithful witnesses of the terrible iniquity which had come under their observation, and readily impose their illusions on the credulous world.

Rival sects, rival parties, and rival nations, are very much inclined to slander each other in these days of enlightenment, and it is not to be supposed that they would manifest a charitable disposition and refrain from all misrepresentation when struggling for ascendancy in a ruder age. The Nazarenes were probably not more addicted to calumny than the generality of their contemporaries. When Joseph of Arimathæa and his associates were plotting to bring the Sanhedrin into discredit, there were plenty of other zealots who would have been ready enough to incriminate their opponents by similar means if placed in like circumstances. When Paul and his successors went from city to city preaching the Gospel, and holding up the Jewish rulers to reprobation for purely imaginary crimes, they occasionally encountered a great deal of detraction themselves. They were vilified by unscrupulous opponents; to injure their reputation abominable stories were circulated in which there was not an atom of truth. Some ecclesiastical historians have been careful to show that the early Christians suffered from calumny without making mention of their own persistent slanders. Canon Robertson, writing of the period A.D. 98-138, says:—

"Strange and horrible charges began to be current against the Christians. The secrecy of their meetings for worship was ascribed, not to its true cause, the fear of persecution, but to a consciousness of abominations which could not bear the light. 'Thyestian banquets,' promiscuous intercourse of the sexes, and magical rites were popularly imputed to them. The Jews were especially industrious in inventing and propagating such stories; some of the heretical parties which now began to vex the Church, both brought discredit on the Christian name by their own practices, and were forward to join in the work of slander and persecution against the faithful" ("History of the Christian Church," Book I., p. 9).

That the Jews at this period should have made unfounded charges against the Christians, and thus helped to bring discredit on them, is not at all to be wondered at considering how the rival community, which was proselytising in every direction, had calumniated them. They felt convinced that the stories which were being propagated among the credulous Gentile population about the extraordinary birth of Jesus, his miracles, his crucifixion, and his rising from the dead, were untruthful, yet so obscure had been his existence that they could get no authentic information about him to refute these legends. They did, therefore, what was frequently done by people at that time in like circumstances; they endeavoured to defeat one falsehood by starting another; to overthrow the fictions of their opponents, they introduced fables of a totally contrary character. "The Sepher Toldoth Jeschu" and other Jewish stories, antagonistic to the high claims of Christianity, thus came into existence, but they were not widely circulated and could do very little harm to the Christian cause.

When two opposing parties resort to calumny as a means of influencing public opinion, that which can furnish stories of cruelty and oppression will have the best chance to succeed. It has been said that during the American Civil War, John Brown and Uncle Tom were, as martyrs, worth a hundred thousand men for animating and strengthening the Northern hostility. In that tremendous fratricidal struggle, both sides went to great lengths in propagating slander, but the calumnies in reference to the Southern planters, who lorded it over poor slaves, could not fail to have most effect with a democratic population passionately devoted to freedom. In our own country, legislation has recently been directed against the lies which are often told on the eve of a political election for the purpose of prejudicing an adverse cause in the eyes of the more ignorant and credulous voters. A charge of immorality on such an occasion is worth much less than a charge of tyranny; a candidate who happens to be a magistrate or an employer of labour, residing at a distance, is the most sure to suffer from partisan calumny. So when the Jews and Christians long ago met as rival propagandists, and were asking for the world's suffrages, they damaged each other's prospects as far as possible by spreading defamatory reports. But the Christians had this great advantage in the conflict of aspersion, that they were able to denounce the Jews as a proud ruling aristocracy, exercising much tyranny at Jerusalem, while holding Jesus up, at the same time, as the victim of their monstrous injustice. Nothing would take better with those in a humble, impoverished condition than a pathetic story, setting forth how Jesus came with a message from Heaven, yet was despised by men of learning, hated and persecuted by proud magistrates, and, at length, subjected to an ignominious death. It was this matchless martyr device that trumped all other devices, and won the election for them; it was this that brought in the multitudinous converts, and gave the Church, at length, her overwhelming majority.

Nothing has ever been known to equal martyrdom as a moving force in religious and political struggles, and there is little wonder at its being so often simulated for that purpose. In times of fierce excitement a mysterious suicide has occasionally furnished means of incriminating a party, and directing against it popular resentment. The death of Sir Edmondsbury Godfrey, the "Protestant martyr," in the reign of Charles II. is generally considered a case of this description. That gentleman had received in his magisterial capacity the lying depositions of Titus Oates respecting the alleged Popish Plot, and was soon after found dead in a ditch near Primrose Hill, with a sword thrust through his body. The Papists were at once suspected and accused of having murdered him, and a tremendous sensation was produced throughout the country. Hume says:—

"In order to propagate the popular frenzy, several artifices were employed. The dead body of Godfrey was carried into the city, attended by vast multitudes; it was publicly exposed in the streets, and viewed by all ranks of men; and everyone who saw it went away inflamed, as well by the mutual contagion of sentiment as by the dismal spectacle itself. The funeral pomp was celebrated with great parade; the corpse was conducted through the chief streets of the city. Seventy-two clergymen marched before; above a thousand persons of distinction followed after; and at the funeral sermon two able-bodied divines mounted the pulpit, and stood on each side of the preacher, lest in paying the last duties to this unhappy magistrate, he should, before the whole people, be murdered by the Papists. In this disposition of the nation, reason could no more be heard, than a whisper in the midst of the most violent hurricane" ("Hist.," lxvii. 4).

Some have expressed the opinion that Godfrey fell by his own hand, or was slain by some other Protestant with the deliberate design of incriminating, and exciting popular feeling against the Papists, since his death occurred so opportunely for that purpose. No direct evidence has been produced in support of this view; but if the magistrate committed suicide, as is now generally believed, he must have foreseen that a great commotion would soon arise, and that the Papists would be suspected of murdering him. Even in our own times many zealots, who have ceased to care much for life, would be well disposed to die in such a way that they might greatly help on a cause to which they are passionately devoted, and be esteemed martyrs by posterity. A remarkable instance of such a sacrifice resolutely contrived to serve party purposes, yet failing at the last moment to be carried out, occurred during the great French Revolution. Lamartine, writing of that fierce struggle, says:—

"There were at this moment (July, 1792) in Paris two men fanatically devoted to their party. . . . Chabot and Grangeneuve were of the Council Chamber of Charenton. One evening they left together one of these conferences, downcast and discouraged by the hesitation and temporising of the conspirators. Grangeneuve was walking with his eyes cast to the ground, and in silence. 'What are you thinking of?' inquired Chabot, 'I was thinking' replied the Girondist, 'that these delays enervate the Revolution and the country. I think that if the people give any time to royalty, they are lost. I think there is but the assigned hour to revolution, and that they who allow it to escape will never recover it, and will owe an account hereafter to God and posterity. Well, Chabot, the people will never rise of themselves—they require some moving power. How is this to be given to them? I have reflected, and at last I think I have discovered the means; but shall I find a man equally capable of the necessary firmness and secrecy to aid me?' 'Speak,' said Chabot, 'I am capable of anything to destroy what I hate.' 'Then,' continued Grangeneuve, 'blood intoxicates the people, there is always pure blood in the cradle of great revolutions, from that of Lucretia to that of William Tell and Sydney. For statesmen, revolutions are a theory; but to the people they are a vengeance, yet to drive them to vengeance we must show them a victim. Since the court refuses us this consolation, we must ourselves immolate it to the cause; a victim must appear to fall beneath the blows of the aristocracy, and it must be some man whom the court shall be supposed to have sacrified, one of its known enemies, and a member of the Assembly, so that the attempt against a national representative may be added in the act to the assassination of a citizen. This assassination must be committed at the very doors of the palace, that it may bring the vengeance down as near as possible. But who shall be this citizen? Myself! I am weak in works; my life is useless to liberty; my death will be of advantage to it; my dead body will be the standard of insurrection and victory to the people!' Chabot listened to Grangeneuve with admiration. 'It is the genius of patriotism that inspires you,' he said 'and if two victims are required, I will be the second.' 'You shall be more than that,' replied Grangeneuve, 'you shall be not the assassin, for I implore you to put me to death, but the priest of the sacrifice. This very night I will walk alone and unarmed, in the most lonely and dark spot near the Louvre; place there two devoted patriots armed with daggers; let us agree on a signal, they shall then stab me, and I will fall without a cry. They will fly. My body will be found next day. You shall accuse the court, and the vengeance of the people will do the rest.' Chabot, as fanatical and as decided as Grangeneuve to calumniate the king by the death of a patriot, swore to his friend that he would commit this odious deceit of vengeance. The rendezvous of the assassination was fixed, the hour appointed, the signal agreed upon. Grangeneuve returned home and made his will, prepared for death, and went at the concerted moment. After walking there for two hours, he saw some men approach, whom he mistook for the appointed assassins. He made the signal agreed upon, and awaited the blow. None was struck. Chabot had hesitated to complete it, either from want of resolution or want of instruments. The victim had not failed for the sacrifice, it was only the slayer" ("History of the Girondists," B. xix. 5).

The crucifixion of Jesus strikingly resembles this contemplated assassination of Grangeneuve in its being a sacrifice contrived by a revolutionary party to have the appearance of a crime. That the nailing and spearing, supposed to have been done by Roman soldiers at the instance of the Sanhedrin, was really executed by servants of his own partisans there cannot be a reasonable doubt. And his sect soon began to reap the advantage which might be expected to result from such a martyr-show in a constantly increasing influx of popular sympathy. What Jesus himself contemplated by a sacrificial death was the fulfilment of Scripture as the suffering Messiah, and a speedy ascension to rule the saints in the Kingdom of Heaven. His partisans, while entertaining the same belief, were desirous as politic men to make his crucifixion serve the further purpose of discrediting the Sanhedrin, and contributing to the growth of the Church. And it must be admitted that they had much knowledge of human nature, that their arrangements were well carried out, and that the persistent holding before the world their case of unparalleled injustice as a means of influencing opinion was attended with immense success.

§ 9.—*The Betraying Manner.*

We have now given several distinct reasons for believing that the crucifixion of Jesus was not a crime or martyrdom as commonly supposed, but a dramatic representation of criminality for party purposes. In support of this view there may be further adduced evidence of a very significant character, to which attention has not yet been directed. When people present illusory appearances to the world for the purpose of influencing opinion, they are generally betrayed, in a while, to intelligent observers by their faulty manner, for they seldom imitate natural conduct in every feature with absolute correctness. Those who are conversant with modern criminal investigations, know well that there are means of distinguishing a genuine charge of guilt from one that is merely got up to serve the accuser's ends. A real crime is concealed with the greatest care, where it is found possible to do so, while the evidences of a pretended crime are made very prominent, so as to attract notice. It is usual for murderers to be at great trouble to hide or destroy all evidences of their guilt, if there is any means of its accomplishment. But in the absurd charges that were formerly got up against the Jews there were sure to be found conspicuous traces of their supposed wickedness. It was made to appear that they were singularly careless in perpetrating atrocities, and sure in some way to incriminate themselves. The children that they crucified on Good Friday were left behind as a ghastly spectacle to horrify all the neighbouring population. In the alleged assaults on the Host, the absence of concealment was still more remarkable, because it would have been easy to dispose of a wafer, but the minute *corpus delicti* was invariably left to tell its tale of guilt, together with the murderous bodkins and awls which had pierced it and drawn blood. Had such cases been submitted to the consideration of an enlightened and impartial judge, he would have been convinced that there were no human beings simple enough to reveal their criminality in that glaring manner, and would have declared that what was represented as being done by the villainous Jews, was really the work of their enemies.

If rulers abuse the power that is entrusted to them, and perpetrate crimes, they are liable to suffer from the popular resentment, and have therefore just as much reason as anyone else to study secrecy and throw a veil over their transgressions. Probably no ruler ever stood in greater fear of the people than poor Louis XVI. in the summer of 1792, when, being shut up as a prisoner in the Louvre, he felt that his life was in constant danger from the violence of the disaffected Parisians. Had he and his advisers under such circumstances deemed it politic to assassinate a hostile member of the National Assembly, they would have felt bound to proceed with the greatest possible caution in carrying out their foul design, and would have taken special care that no trace of their murdered victim should be discovered. Grangeneuve, however, in plotting to incriminate the king for the furtherance of the revolutionary cause, would have made it appear that he was a great deal more daring and unscrupulous in punishing obnoxious persons than his despotic grandfather had ever been, that, in fact, he did not hesitate to kill a member of the Assembly at the very door of his palace, nor mind in the least about the atrocious act obtaining publicity. And had the scheme been carried out without a hitch, although some few might have entertained suspicions as to its contrivance, it would in all probability have raised the people as calculated on; they would have felt certain that their good republican member had fallen under the daggers of court assassins, and proceeded with the greatest fury to avenge his death just as a former generation of prejudiced people had been incited by stratagem to massacre the Jews.

The seventy elders who met in the Temple under the presidency of Gamaliel were not the sort of men likely to engage in a foul murder conspiracy; they could gain nothing, at any rate, by putting Jesus to death; but supposing they had the disposition and the motive to effect his removal, we may be quite sure that they would not have gone about the nefarious business in the way that they are represented as doing by the Evangelists. They would have known, at least, that righteous dealing was expected of them; they would have felt that it was necessary to keep up an appearance of probity in the face of their observant countrymen, and would have been careful to execute their malice against the Prophet of Nazareth in a manner that was unlikely to provoke popular resentment. In ancient times, when persons free from the taint of crime were tried and condemned to death for state reasons, and the justness of their sentence was sure to be disputed by many, it was not usual to make a great parade of their penal sufferings. Socrates was so condemned by a majority of the Athenian Council, but, knowing that he had a host of friends and sympathisers, they did not proceed to torture him and subject him to every conceivable indignity. They were not at all eager to incur the responsibility of taking the life of such a man, but by passing sentence on him, were rather desirous to drive him away from the city. When, however, it was seen that he did not wish to escape death, as they gave him plenty of opportunities of doing, they arranged for him to execute the sentence on himself, and die in a quiet, dignified manner worthy of a philosopher. Nothing was done by his opponents calculated to give unnecessary offence to those who respected his teaching, and cause them to regard his condemnation to death with a feeling of bitter resentment.

Jesus was only a transient visitor at Jerusalem, one of many visitors who flocked to the city at the Passover season; he had never resided there permanently, as Socrates had done at Athens, nor created by his teaching anything like the same amount of disturbance. Still, if the Sanhedrin had been an independent national assembly, and had resolved on condemning him to death, they would have been likely to exhibit some such discretion as that of the Athenian Council in carrying out the sentence. Knowing that Jesus was a popular teacher, it would not have seemed to them wise and politic to crucify him, rather than have him executed by some mild means in the seclusion of a prison. Crucifixion was resorted to by nearly all ancient nations only as a deterrent punishment for very flagrant offences which it was reasonable to apprehend would be repeated. The robber, the murderer, the incendiary, or the insurgent after perpetrating much wrong, and causing great trouble to the community, was at length caught and nailed up, that his wretched fate might thus afford a terrible warning to others. But Jesus was no criminal, and the particular course which he had taken as a teacher was not likely to be followed by anyone else, so that a severe deterrent punishment in his case could serve no good purpose at all. The crucifixion of a harmless prophet would be absurd as a real repressive act of the Jewish authorities; it could have no other effect on the popular mind but the enlistment of sympathy in behalf of the sufferer, and the excitement of indignation against those who, as ministers of justice, could act so unreasonably and perpetrate such terrible wrong.

Not only would it have been monstrous for the Sanhedrin to crucify Jesus, but it would have been extremely unwise to proceed against him judicially and arraign him before the procurator, when it was clear that he had not broken the laws of the country. Had they really deemed it desirable to remove him from their path by violence, while they yet saw no prospect of getting him fairly convicted on any capital charge, they would doubtless have sought to compass his death secretly by assassination. Such has always been the method that unscrupulous rulers have adopted to get rid of dangerous opponents whom they could not prove guilty of any crime. In the seventeenth century, for instance, the Venetian Council of Ten repeatedly sought by poisoning, and other insidious means, to get rid of this and that troublesome agitator when they could not see their way to accomplish that object judicially. As Jesus was a homeless wanderer, often alone or only accompanied by a few unarmed disciples, he must have presented at such times a most accessible mark for assassins. And it would have been far more reasonable to obtain the effective services of such wretches for a small sum of money, than to suborn a number of false witnesses to come and swear away his life. The fact, then, that no attempt at poisoning, no stealthy dagger assault was made on him, that he went where he pleased in the neighbourhood of Jerusalem unmolested, either by night or by day, is a convincing proof that the chief priests and rulers were not, as they have been represented, persistently plotting and seeking how they might by subtlety take and put him to death. For they never would have been such fools as to hazard open judicial proceedings for the attainment of their foul purpose, nor incurred the obloquy of unjustly delivering one of their countrymen into the hands of the Romans to be crucified when they could, with so much more advantage, have secretly struck him down, or at least, attempted to do so in his retirement.

While it is extremely improbable that the Jewish rulers would entertain the idea of crucifying a popular teacher like Jesus, their perpetration of such a flagrant outrage in open day without encountering any serious opposition would have been absolutely impossible. The easy way in which the alleged judicial murder is said to have been accomplished, the absence of all interruption to the terrible tragedy, furnishes the clearest proof that the opponents of Jesus had nothing to do with it, and could only have been present in dramatic appearance.

A murder or robbery has now and then been committed where fierce and vigilant dogs were kept ever ready to give notice of the approach of intruders, and yet those faithful watchers were silent at the time. People have rightly inferred from this that the perpetrator of the offence must be one of the household, since no stranger would have been able to control the animals, and prevent them from making a loud demonstration of hostility. So when we see how resistance to the Crucifixion was marvellously charmed away, we are driven to infer that it was not the work of external foes, but a domestic performance of the Nazarenes. It is very clear that no one had the power to prevent a tremendous outburst of indignation against the cruel wrong which was apparently being done, but the Nazarene leaders themselves. Joseph of Arimathæa could have easily exercised a becalming and restraining influence over the disciples, such as it would not have been possible for any hostile Jews to accomplish under the direction of Joseph Caiaphas. We know that they were not prevented from speaking their minds by the fear of enemies, and silence could only have been imposed on them by the persuasion of friends, by some private inspirations which have not been revealed in the report of the Evangelists.

Assuming the crucifixion of Jesus to be a crime, the whole transaction, as reported in the Gospels, is quite as discreditable to Christians as it is to Jews.

If the Sanhedrin or any other body of men were wickedly conspiring to take his life, it would have been the duty of his followers to contend with these enemies, and do all in their power to effect his deliverance. Yet it appears that they simply looked on as passive spectators, and suffered the iniquitous proceedings which were being directed against him to take their course. Any behaviour, under the circumstances, more shameful and scandalous than theirs it is scarcely possible to conceive. We are told that while Pilate, the supreme judge in the matter, believed in the innocence of Jesus, and manifested a very strong desire to save him, not one of those who regarded him as their master and friend would step forward to speak a word in his favour, and ask that he should be acquitted. A monstrous crime was about to be perpetrated, and they were consenting parties to it, as they would not so much as turn a straw for its prevention. When the foul deed was at length accomplished they took no steps to prosecute and bring to justice the murderers. These wicked plotters, instead of being impeached before the Roman senate, together with Pilate for allowing himself to be made their tool, were permitted to go to their graves in peace. Then, having acquiesced in this terrible atrocity, and suffered the guilty to go scot free, they began to raise a howl of Christ-murder against the innocent portion of the community, and bring on them the wholly undeserved hatred and execration of mankind.

An apology is now frequently made for the base conduct of the followers of Jesus in not having pleaded for him or exerted themselves resolutely to save his life. We are told that they offered no resistance to the nefarious plot which was being carried out before their eyes, because his death had been foretold, and they were assured that it was absolutely necessary for him to suffer as Messiah in fulfilment of Scripture. But this is not a valid justification of their behaviour on the supposition that they witnessed the perpetration of a terrible wrong which might have been prevented. Kings, presidents, and other public men have now and then been assassinated after it was several times predicted that they would die by violence, and their friends have not been influenced by such predictions to neglect doing all that could be done for their protection and safety. If the attendants of a murdered prince were to avow that they made no attempt to defend him because it had been said that he would suffer in such a way, and they were fully convinced in their own minds that it was decreed by Providence, such a plea would not avail in the least to excuse their culpable dereliction of duty.

But the true apology for the disciples and sympathisers of Jesus in not interposing to save him from crucifixion is, that they thereby acted in accordance with his wishes, for he made no attempt to save himself. It was clearly on his part a voluntary act of suffering, an ordeal which he deliberately prepared to undergo after consulting with his friends, and not a cruel punishment forced on him unawares by designing enemies. Had he felt aggrieved at what was being done, and desired to be delivered from a hostile assault, there would not have been wanting outside the circle of his immediate followers plenty to rally to his support. There can be no doubt that Jesus, although not widely known, was a popular teacher, the propounders of communistic doctrines always have been popular with the lowest and poorest classes of men. The general equalisation and distribution of human possessions which he advocated, would have so endeared him to the multitude, that his friends could not fail to outnumber his foes. Those who are responsible for maintaining order, have generally been reluctant to lay hold of such a teacher only to imprison him for a short time, unless his proceedings seemed likely to cause serious mischief. Imagine, then, a harmless advocate of human equality being seized in the midst of a sympathetic population, and publicly crucified! Treatment so grossly outrageous, inflicted on one who had committed no crime, and had contantly pleaded for the poor, could not fail to incense and exasperate the multitude. And when we are told that Jesus was taken and dealt with in this cruel manner without any such result following, without so much as provoking a whisper of disapprobation, we know that he was simply sacrificed according to his desires, and in agreement with what were considered the interests of the Nazarene community. For the Jewish rulers to have determined on the Crucifixion as a militant stroke against a sect notoriously animated with the martyr-spirit, they would have committed a blunder only possible for people in a condition of absolute madness; but viewed as a dramatic act of warfare on the part of the Nazarenes it was a well-concerted measure, indicating that some among that body possessed a considerable amount of astuteness.

§ 10.—*The Conclusion.*

Those who place themselves in opposition to an ancient, strongly-rooted belief held by many millions of people, must not expect by much controversy to make any perceptible impression on them or produce any great immediate results. No amount of argument will induce the majority of mankind to abandon established myths, however prejudicial or unreasonable, but they are sure to give way gradually to the growth of intelligence. Enlightened Christians, as they continually acquire larger views and broader sympathies, will not be able much longer to believe in the diabolical wickedness of the Jewish rulers as their forefathers might well do in the days of witchcraft. A governing body so utterly abominable and lost to all sense of probity and verity as the Temple magistracy are made to appear, could not exist in Jerusalem or anywhere else. No people in the world would allow the administration of justice to be in the hands of a set of bloodthirsty miscreants far more vile than any ordinary gang of thieves. The Crucifixion story of the Evangelists may be held more stoutly than their Gehenna doctrines; it will not be lightly thrust aside by criticism as the mediæval stories of martyred children have been, on account of the immense structure of sacrificial superstition since erected upon it by the Church. But this superstition is now visibly on the decline, it will go the way, at length, of the older notion which it superseded, that of purchasing redemption from sin with the blood of oxen and goats, and then the reformed Jew and the reformed Christian, meeting on the basis of the two great commandments—Love of God and Love of Humanity—will join hands and be thoroughly reconciled.

Some people, who have never taken the trouble to investigate the subject, tell us that the great criminal charge against the Jews would have been long ago disproved if it had not rested on a good foundation. It is very unreasonable to presume that such should be the case; a false accusation is by no means certain to break down or meet with speedy exposure; evidence to overthrow it is not always obtainable, and even if it should be demonstrated groundless, the popular belief in it may be obstinately maintained. The early Christians who first set out from Jerusalem and reported the Crucifixion among Gentile communities were under the great advantage of having no opposition to encounter; they told their incriminating story to the ignorant and credulous and were readily believed. They did, indeed, meet with a few Jews occasionally who regarded them as calumniators, but such opponents, having no knowledge of the alleged criminal transaction, were unable to refute their statement and prevent it from obtaining further credit. The accusation, therefore, continually gained ground, and got to be considered at length a well-established historical truth throughout the greater part of the Roman Empire. When Christianity had once acquired a dominant position in the world, the Jews, who still disbelieved in the terrible allegations made against the Sanhedrin, were compelled to maintain a discreet silence. If they had ventured on publishing books, which called in question the extraordinary statements of the Evangelists, they must have answered for such temerity with their lives. It is only in comparatively recent times that toleration has so far advanced as to permit them to criticise the Gospels, and openly vindicate their religious position. And, as might be expected, modern Jews are not very ready and eager to take advantage of this liberty; they have no proselytising ambition, and controversy with Christians is considered impolitic and greatly discouraged throughout their community. Their own journals depend, to some extent, on the support of Christian subscribers, to whom it is not well to give any needless offence. Now and then an article, such as the following, appears in reference to "The Crucifixion: "—

"The discovery of the mischief which the incessant reiteration of this charge (Deicide) inflicts on the Jews is not new. It was made by them at the very moment Christianity ascended the throne of the Roman world. And here shines forth conspicuously the liberality of our age. For fifteen centuries the Jews knew, and terribly felt, the consequences of this charge. But they were never permitted to examine it, or, if examine, to state the result arrived at. A charge repeated from generation to generation and never refuted, was naturally considered irrefutable by those who propagated it. It was only after the lapse of fifteen centuries that those so wofully affected by the charge were permitted to publish the result of their inquiries. What the liberality of the age permitted, its practical tendencies impelled some of the leading minds of those concerned to undertake. Here we have the reasons for this important discussion reserved for our age. . . . . . Will these temperate discussions of eminent co-religionists be productive of the desired result? Not immediately, but eventually. The civilised world has unlearned so many prejudices, that we need not despair of seeing it conquer those against the Jewish race. Among the laity there are now thousands ready to listen to arguments and accept the results of sound criticism. In proportion as this readiness spreads among the laity, it also forces itself upon the clergy. With the tact which distinguishes large classes of them, they will soon discover that the senseless charges of bygone ages, even if brought forward in a milder form, are no longer palatable to the mass sufficiently reasonable to see their uncritical nature, and sufficiently moral to perceive their hideousness. The clergy and the teachers will then no longer dwell so unctuously and emphatically on those portions of the Christian records which seem to favour these lamentable charges, but rather upon those which recommend peace and goodwill upon all men. This process of pacification may be a slow one. It may require years before an impression can be produced sufficiently deep and widespread to be perceived, but we must not flag in our efforts" (*Jewish Chronicle*).

We entirely agree with this temperate article excepting in one point; it seems to us that a large portion of the clergy are far better prepared than the great mass of the laity to reconsider the whole case against the Jews, and correct the extremely uncharitable and calumnious disposition of the primitive Church. It must be said to the credit of many good Christian ministers, that their improved exposition of the Gospels at the present day is gradually enlightening people, and effecting no inconsiderable reform. They throw out no hint calculated to weaken the authority of those narratives, but they contrive to moderate their Diabolism to a great extent, to soften their harsh tone in reference to the Jewish rulers, and read into them a more generous and charitable spirit. The grim, distorted faces of the old caricature are, under their skilful hands, retouched in such a manner that they lose their repulsiveness and come to be recognised as the features of our fellow-men. They also freely acknowledge the mistakes which were made by the primitive Church in reference to forged Apocalyptic writings, and the numerous types and predictions which were supposed to point to Jesus as the Messiah. And while they thus exhibit the ancient rulers of Israel in a much better light than that under which they have hitherto been viewed by the Church, they never fail to speak respectfully of their modern Jewish neighbours and fellow-citizens, whom they regard as conscientious religionists standing on the same moral level as themselves. They also lose no opportunity of strongly denouncing the persecutions directed against the Jews in other lands, and the disabilities to which they are subjected through the lingering there of ancient prejudice. Let them only persevere in these generous efforts, and they will atone for much wrong that has been done in the past, and bring about an improved relationship and a true fraternal feeling highly beneficial to both communities. Dean W. H Fremantle, in a sympathetic article on progressive

Judaism, after showing the great services which the Jews rendered the Church in helping on the Reformation, writes as follows:—

"There are two powerful influences which draw men together in modern society and which become more and more a part of religion. One of these is literature, the other social and political life. The Jewish race opens itself out freely to both these influences. It has no doubt a certain literature of its own, but not probably more extensive than that of several of the religious sects. . . . . But the history, the poetry, the philosophy, even the biography of a Christian nation is as much the inheritance of its Jewish as of its Gentile members; and the influence of literature upon morals and religion grows with the growth of education. It is the solvent of all systems and creeds, and the bond of their higher unity. And the same may be said even in a higher degree of social and political life; for the relations of men to one another, whether as individuals or in classes and communities, cannot be dissociated from religion. It is as truly a part of religion as is the worship of God. When men find themselves constantly pursuing, side by side, the same philanthropic objects, acting together as members of the same societies, speaking out and sharing together their deepest convictions in questions of vast importance to themselves and their fellow-men, when they have struggled side by side and on the same ground for the success of a great cause, and have come to adopt the same standard of moral judgment, it is hardly possible that these men should be truly said to be of different religions" (*Contemporary Review*, Vol. XXXII., p. 785).

It would be well if such broad and liberal Christian teaching were more general at the present day; far more good would result from it than will ever be accomplished by pestering the Jews with sermons preached to effect their conversion. Unfortunately, a large class of ministers have not yet attained to this enlightenment; there is a strong disposition manifested in some Churches to revive the superstitious feeling of mediæval times, rather than to make further progress. Where the subject of the Crucifixion is much dwelt upon and Good Friday is kept as a day of terrible gloom, it is scarcely possible that any friendly feeling should subsist between Christians and Jews. Moreover, the fits of asceticism that are fostered in this way, are not by any means conducive to a sound and healthy morality. The female sex, as might be expected, offer the greatest encouragement to sacerdotal charms and all kinds of religious excitements. Hundreds of ladies who lead idle and frivolous lives, after going through a round of pleasure, will kneel before a crucifix and shed penitential tears, when they ought to be studying how to become good and useful members of society. Religion is to them, not a reformation of evils habits, but a system of frequent medicine-taking to drive away the maladies that are sure to come from much vicious indulgence.

One remarkable instance of retrogressive teaching calculated to revive the old hostility between Jews and Christians, is furnished by a recent religious tale entitled "Barabbas." Miss Marie Corelli, the talented authoress of this work, thinks that the Jewish rulers, who happened to be contemporary with Jesus, so far from being outrageously maligned, have not been painted half black enough in the Evangelical narratives. And she sets out as one newly inspired to improve on their work of vilification in a sort of Fifth Gospel which she has thus placed before the world. She is convinced that the fierce flogging, the blood-curdling cruelty practised on the Prophet of Nazareth by his religious opponents, has been passed over by the old writers with too light a hand, and therefore she pictures the scene vividly, as she thinks it likely to have been, in all its horrifying details. It further appears to her that those wicked Jewish rulers were capable of every imaginable villainy, and must have committed numerous crimes which were forgotten or not put on record. As no mention seems to have been made of their lewdness, she thinks it right, in strict justice, to depict them as being not only cruel but grossly sensual, and under a garb of religious sanctity carrying on an iniquitous practice of debauchery and intrigue. In describing the Crucifixion she says:—

"At the crafty suggestion of Caiaphas, the two thieves who had been brought out from prison that morning were nailed on their respective crosses first. This was to satisfy the refined cruelty of the Jewish priests, who by this means sought to overpower the 'Nazarene' with terror by forcing Him to witness the agonies of those who were destined to suffer in His sacred company. But herein the bloodthirsty chiefs of the Sanhedrin were doomed to disappointment. No shadow of fear blanched the serene visage of the Divine, not a tremor of horror or anxiety quivered through that stately frame of heroic stature and perfect mould. He stood erect as a king of a thousand worlds might stand, conscious of power and glory. His tall white-robed figure was fully outlined against the burning sky, and seemed to have gathered from the sunrays a dazzling luminance of its own—every prickly point in His crown of thorns glistened as with drops of dew—His fair calm face shone with a beauty not of mortals, and so lightly did His sandalled feet seem poised on the hot and arid soil beneath Him, that He scarcely appeared to touch the earth more than a sunlit cloud may do ere rising again into its native ether. The land, the sky, the air, the sun, all seemed to be a part of Himself and to share mysteriously in the knowledge of His presence; had

He spoken one word—one word of thunderous command, it would have shaken the Universe! . . . Presently a loud roar of ferocious delight went up from the mob, the executioners had stripped the condemned of His garments. . . . The select and richly-attired company of those influential or wealthy persons who were standing immediately round the high priest, Caiaphas, now advanced a little, Judith Iscariot (the wicked mistress of Caiaphas), radiant as a sunflash embodied in woman's shape, leaned forward eagerly, with the pleased smile of a child who is promised some rare and mirthful gala show. Her brilliant dark eyes roved indifferently and coldly over the outstretched Form upon the Cross—her jewelled vest rose and fell lightly with the gradual excited quickening of her breath. She looked, but she did not speak, she seemed to gloat silently on the prospect of the blood-shedding and torture soon to ensue" (pp. 116, 130, 132).

If this Gospel according to Marie had been written at Ephesus, Antioch, or some other Asiatic town in the beginning of the second century, it would doubtless have been considered an inspired production and would have obtained an honoured place among the authoritative records of the Church. Even in this intelligent and critical age it has met with much approval and obtained a wide circulation among the more credulous and sensation-loving portion of the Christian community. The authoress, speaking proudly of her success and the great encouragement which she had received from Canon Wilberforce and others, in the *Idler* of February, 1895, says, that fourteen editions of "Barabbas" have been published, consisting of more than thirty thousand copies, and that the book "has made its position, not only among English-speaking peoples, but also on the continent through the medium of translation into six different

European languages, besides having penetrated to the furthest East in the Parsi dialect and in Hindustani." She goes on to set forth her aim in writing the work. "Upon the careless, the cynical, and the forgetful, I sought to impress, through the medium of romance, as I would through any other means that lay in my power, a vivid picture of the reality of Christ's existence upon earth, and to bring close to the imagination of the reader the human and Divine intention of His life and death. Because I see and know that though the sublime New Testament story is read diligently at all our sacred services, there are no people more ignorant of its high meaning, its majestic philosophy and spiritual comfort, than the regular and fashionable church-goers. Paradoxical as this sounds, it is nevertheless true, and a reason for it is not far to seek. The monotonous reading of the Gospel by our clergy, who, with a few notable exceptions, are the worst elocutionists in the world, would take all life and meaning out of the grandest prose or poetry extant. The sing-song drawl, the sameness of tone, the want of proper accentuation and emphasis, and what is more regrettable than anything, *the lack of love and heart in the reading;* these deaden and drown the simple and sonorous rhythm of the Holy Text, and make the wonderful life-lessons of the Divine Master seem merely tiresome repetitions of moral platitudes. So much so, indeed, that even the magnificent Gospel selections for Good Friday often fail in their intended effect. . . .

"I should like to say how great a part of my reward is found in the fact that everywhere, not only among differing sects, but also among creeds that have nothing in common with Christianity, the ideal figure of Christ which I have drawn—with how much love and reverence none can know—has taken with it unanimous conviction, and awakened an equally unanimous response. The general impression among the readers of 'Barabbas' is, that they realise Christ more clearly, and are drawn in more intimate and devout relations with the scenes of the majestic tragedy enacted on Calvary."

And no doubt the readers of " Barabbas " realise, at the same time, more clearly the diabolical wickedness of the Jewish people; they are enabled to understand, as they never did before, the terrible love of cruelty inherent in that accursed race. During the Middle Ages the martyr ballads which were written in commemoration of crucified children, and the paintings representing those horrid outrages which were exhibited in public places served a very similar purpose. It was usual in such works of art to depict a sweet Christian child stretched out crosswise on a table surrounded by a number of fierce, malignant Jews who were preparing to torture it with their knives. People had heard that the Jews were capable of these fiendish atrocities, but when they came to look on a picture of that kind they could fully realise it all, they felt as though they had actually been present and had witnessed the crimes. And they were consequently all the more ready to believe in any evil report which was got up against the Jews of their neighbourhood, and join in a senseless howl for bringing down vengeance on their supposed blood-guiltiness. " Barabbas," as a calumnious work of art, may be expected to have the same pernicious influence; it is not likely to do much harm in this country, but, being so widely circulated and translated into six different European languages, it is pretty sure to strengthen the inveterate anti-Jewish prejudice which exists in some parts of the Continent. And the immense success of the book is likely to encourage other writers of fiction to attempt something of the same kind, so as to perhaps even exceed its exaggerations of ancient calumnies. People will not have the least inclination to imitate Miss Corelli's Divine Christ, but very many will be moved by the pictures which she has drawn, to entertain a strong Jew-hatred, and imitate the vindictive acts of the Crusaders.

Professor Graetz and other modern Jewish scholars have expressed a very favourable opinion of Jesus; they believe him to have been a decidedly more estimable character than he is made to appear in the narrative of the Evangelists. An enlightened Christian poet or novelist, dealing freely with his life, would be likely to take the same view, and would endeavour as far as possible to correct the errors and misrepresentations of his early biographers. He would present us with an edifying human picture of the Galilean prophet going forth to admonish his countrymen and labouring as a peacemaker to heal their strifes. Miss Corelli, instead of writing a Gospel of Reconciliation, has done the very reverse; she has produced a story which is calculated to force two great kindred communities that have been set at variance, further apart than ever. Her notion of improving on the Evangelists is precisely that of the second-century writers; there is always some hope of divided brethren who stand on the same level effecting a *rapprochement*, but by making Jesus more divine, and the Jews more diabolical, she has endeavoured, as far as possible, to establish between their respective followers a perpetual estrangement.

Christian poets have occasionally sought to enlarge and embellish the Gospel narrative as the authoress of "Barabbas" has done, and they have generally imparted to it a more gentle and refined modern spirit. A great deal may be said in favour of such attempts as theirs, but what they might venture on doing with far more confidence of good results would be, to write from inspiration some account of the unknown life of Christ. From the age of twenty to thirty, that is, in the period of vigorous early manhood which preceded his coming under Essene influences, and receiving the baptism of John, he is said to have resided quietly with his family at Nazareth, and worked as a carpenter. It may be safely inferred that this was really the best and brightest period of his existence. While he toiled peacefully at Nazareth, his example and the words which occasionally fell from his lips may reasonably be supposed to have much worth for Christian society as now constituted, and the many thousands of people who are placed in similar circumstances. His early biographers, by simply going to Nazareth and making inquiries, might have gleaned a large amount of information respecting this portion of his career if they had chosen to do so, but they were looking eagerly for the approaching end of the world, and evidently thought that nothing which he said and did was worth recording till after he had put down his tools. We have, as the result of their negligence, a great blank left, which might be profitably filled up by Christian poets who are in sympathy with orderly human industry. If they would give us a story of the good son of Joseph, the good brother, the good neighbour, working peacefully at his trade, and assisting and encouraging other workers, their narrative would be read with advantage, not only by Christians, but by Jews; and the two communities, which have been inflamed and set at variance by other writings, might thus to some extent become reconciled.

BY THE SAME AUTHOR.

THE HISTORY OF HEROD:
Another look at a Man emerging from Twenty Centuries of Calumny.

Cloth, 8vo. Price 6s.

"Although the writer adds no new matter to the story told by Josephus, and although he takes the part of an advocate rather than that of a judge, yet his reading of the text is so fair, and the consequent inferences are so reasonable, that he may justly be held to have earned for his client the favourable verdict of posterity. . . . . None but an able soldier, a consummate diplomatist, and a just statesman could have acquired, as Herod undoubtedly did, the confidence of the successive rulers of the Roman world, and the respect of his subjects, as evinced by the tranquillity of his kingdom during the greater part of a long reign, and the anarchy which followed his death. . . . . Our thanks are due to Mr. Vickers for having produced an exceedingly lively and well-written account of the epoch."—*Westminster Review.*

"There can be no doubt that one will be better able to jugde intelligently not only of Herod as a man and a ruler, but also of the Jewish nation from the time of the return from Babylon to its final overthrow by the Romans, after reading this book. In the case of a ruler whose reputation has come to us only through the word of bitter enemies, it is but fair to cross-examine the witnesses."—*The Unitarian* (Chicago).

"To all impressed with the justice of the ancient aphorism, 'Audi alteram partem,' we would commend the perusal of this really remarkable volume."—*Knowledge*.

"Readers of biography and students of history are much indebted to Mr. Vickers for this contribution towards a better understanding of a great man, who has certainly come in for far more than the average share of misrepresentation and calumny always dogging the steps of eminent men in every rank of life. . . . . The 'Introduction' is a masterly *résumé* of the whole case for Herod. The following passage from it is a fair specimen of the author's style and mode of conducting his argument:—

"Alexander, Cæsar, Cromwell, Peter, Frederic, Napoleon, are all ably assailed at the present day and ably defended, just as they were in lifetime, so that between friends and foes they continue to have a fair trial, and no injustice is likely to be done to their reputation. Herod the Great, while living, stood more favourably in general public estimation than most of these; he was highly respected by the foremost men in the world— the men who founded the Roman Empire; his government was the subject of much commendation on three continents; his friends, all the time he reigned over Palestine, decidedly outnumbered his enemies; yet the revolutionary changes which set in after his death, and the monstrous calumnies which were heaped upon him, multiplied the latter year by year and diminished the former, till eventually he had not a friend left. Consequently, instead of receiving anything like fair treatment at the hands of posterity, he has had to run a tremendous gauntlet of protracted hostility, being universally cursed and execrated, assailed from every side as by a fierce unreasoning mob, and not defended at all. Admitting the truth of every evil thing that has been said against him; granting that he was an extremely bad man, a cruel tyrant, a heartless oppressor, a wholesale murderer; his memory is still subjected to a shameful injustice only worthy of the ages of persecution, so long as we see his bad actions constantly paraded before the world in the darkest colours, while all the good which he did is carefully kept out of sight.'"—*The Inquirer*.

www.ingramcontent.com/pod-product-compliance
Lightning Source LLC
Chambersburg PA
CBHW031831230426
43669CB00009B/1309